Thorns of the Lotus

The Eaters of the Lotus Sourcebook

FENG SHUI
Action Movie Roleplaying

by Rich Warren

Credits

"THORNS OF THE LOTUS"

AN ATLAS GAMES PRODUCTION

WRITTEN BY RICH WARREN PUBLISHED BY JOHN NEPHEW

EDITING & LAYOUT BY JOHN NEPHEW AND WILL HINDMARCH

PROOFREAD BY MICHELLE A. B. NEPHEW COVER ART KAGAN MCLEOD

INTERIOR ART BRIAN FIGUR, BRENDON & BRIAN FRAIM, HEATHER HUDSON, GREY THORNBERRY, CHAD SERGESKETTER AND MATT WILSON

DAEDALUS EDITION EDITORIAL & PRODUCTION TEAM JOSE GARCIA, MARIA GARCIA, DANIEL GELON AND JOHN TYNES

ATLAS GAMES SPECIAL THANKS NICOLE LINDROOS

ATLAS GAMES
PO BOX 131233
ROSEVILLE, MN 55113

INFO@ATLAS-GAMES.COM

VISIT US ONLINE AT

WWW.ATLAS-GAMES.COM

ISBN 1-58978-028-0

Table of Contents

Chapter 1

Hoi Mao Qian, son of Hoi Zi Yun, stared at the rolling hills and wheat fields above him. His road cut through these hills. A thousand years of passing wagons ground out a trench deep enough to swallow his cart. He was a simple farmer, not particularly pious, but the Hoi ancestors smiled on him. They blessed him with many sons and many daughters. They brought the gentle rain, giving Zi Yun bountiful harvests.

What's more, misfortune seemed to avoid Zi Yun. Last summer's fire stopped short of his fields, and even the blood-drinking Hsiung-nu avoided his land – raiding neighboring villages instead.

Soon, Zi Yun's small farm grew into a sprawling estate. An estate that Mao Qian's brothers would someday inherit. They would raise families of their own, while his sisters married into other prosperous households.

But Mao would have nothing.

With each bump of the carriage, Mao could feel the dull throbbing between his legs – a wound more than one week old. He remembered his father's order, and the doctor's swift cut that changed him from man to eunuch. Now he traveled south to Lo-yang and the Imperial Palace. He had traveled for six days.

As they crested the hill, Mao saw the great walls of Lo-yang rising in the distance. The driver, an Imperial messenger, whipped the horses forward. More roads joined theirs, like rivers rushing toward the ocean. Soon, they reached the main gates – each large enough for three wagons to pass side-by-side.

Inside, storefronts and temples lined the wide streets. Crowds of finely-dressed people filled the roadways. The driver's shouts sent them scurrying as the coach rattled across the brick surface, but Mao hardly noticed. Anger simmered within him. Anger at his father, jealousy for his brothers. He had bowed to his father's will, like a dutiful son. Yet now he was no longer a man – no longer a son.

The coach shimmied to a stop inside a large courtyard. Mao could hear the messenger unfastening his chests and tossing them carelessly off the back of the carriage. He could see three plump men in finely-embroidered silk, walking out to greet him. His own cheeks burned, as he fingered the coarse woven hemp of his own clothing.

The door to the coach opened, and the first eunuch stepped in. The silk rustled around him, and the scent of lilac oil filled the air. He spoke in a high, shrill voice. "Can this frail urchin be our new arrival, Hoi Mao Qian?"

Mao rose and, keeping his gaze down at his feet, bowed dutifully. "This unworthy servant has traveled from the northern frontier to join the Emperor's household...at his father's request."

The eunuch giggled like a young girl. "Look at this boy. He is of no use to us, except maybe for scrubbing chamber pots. Ah, but he is ours now. I may as well show him his new quarters." The eunuch smiled viciously, then stepped out of the carriage.

Mao swallowed and bit his lower lip. He kept his head bowed, in a show of obedience, but his hands balled into tight fists. "I will remember this, Father." He whispered through clenched teeth. "Some day I will return."

CHAPTER 1

Introduction to the Empire

In the beginning there was neither heaven nor earth. Only chaos, sitting like a hen's egg. But all eggs carry the seed of life, and this seed soon grew into Pangu — the first man. Like a chick cracking its shell he burst into existence, separating the chaos. Heavy elements fell, becoming the earth, while pure ones flew, becoming the sky. These are Yin and Yang.

For eighteen thousand years, the sky and earth separated, growing ten feet farther apart each day. Pangu grew at the same rate, always filling the distance between. Then, upon his death, his body collapsed, becoming the world we know.

His breath formed the wind and clouds, his voice thunder and lighting. His left eye became the sun, his right the moon. The five great mountains grew from his body, while his blood and fluids filled the rivers and seas. His nervous and venous systems formed the layers of the earth. The fields and soil derived from his flesh. His hair and eyebrows became the stars and planets. His teeth and bones became metal and stone; his semen, pearls; his bone marrow, jade. His sweat now falls as rain, and his fleas grew into the human race.

I am Xia Tian Yu. Sit, impudent child, and listen. You have much to learn, if you wish to join the ranks of the Lotus. We have mastered the secrets of true power, seizing control of this world. You will either join us, or you will become our slave. It is your choice — a choice given to very few.

History

Since the day of creation, it has been the role of man to bring order from chaos.

In the ancient past, animals ruled the world. We were few and they were many. Then the Three Sovereigns and the Five Sage Emperors arrived. They taught our ancestors the first secrets and our prosperity followed. Fu Xi invented the eight trigrams, important to both sorcerers and seers. Shen Nong added agriculture and herbal medicine. The Yellow Emperor taught both writing and weapons. Yu the Great tamed the floods.

So it continued until the Virtuous Emperor Yao abdicated his throne in favor of the wise commoner Shun.

Shun, unwilling to place himself among the Sage Emperors, took the title of King and founded the Xia dynasty. Four hundred years of prosperity followed, but eventually the Xia kings grew corrupt and greedy. Heaven withdrew its support, savaging the lands with floods and disasters. Revolution spread, ending only after Tang killed Jie the Wicked and founded the Shang dynasty.

Though the Shang kings conquered much of the steppes, they too grew corrupt, and the mandate from heaven shifted to Zhou — a frontier chief. The Zhou dynasty lasted for seven hundred years and produced many great scholars, including Confucius and Lao Tzu. But the Zhou kings were weak. Invaders conquered their land, and eventually the empire dissolved into a tangle of warring states.

Xia Tain Yu, elder eunuch

Attributes: Bod 3 (Tgh 8), Chi 0 (Mag 6), Mnd 9, Ref 7
Skills: Deceit 14, Info/Chinese History 16, Info/Lotus Bureaucracies 14, Info/Lotus History 14, Info/Lotus Politics 14, Info/Supernatural Creatures 13, Leadership 16, Sorcery 16
Sorcery Schticks: Blast (Acid, Disease, Disintegration, Transmutation), Divination, Influence, Summoning
Unique Schtick
Aura of the Teacher: Xia Tain Yu gains a measure of influence over everyone he instructs — which includes all but the earliest Lotus sorcerers. He gets a +2 AV on all Influence schtick rolls against past and current pupils.
Notes: The narrator of this chapter is one of Gao Zhang's first recruits. Though Xia Tain Yu quickly gained substantial sorcerous power, his true genius lies in his ability to mold others. Since the Lotus's earliest days, Xia has directed the initiation of new sorcerers. His words shape the Lotus's future.

Twin sicknesses eat at the bowels of the Han dynasty: the corruption of the imperial bureaucracy, and the blatant manipulations by the palace eunuchs. As these diseases spread, they infect everyone they touch, turning minds away from their duties and responsibilities. A growing lust for pleasure eats away at the rightful hierarchies, threatening to toss everything into chaos.

Our knowledge of the future has shown that heaven will soon notice these earthly excesses. Its mandate will shift, and the Han dynasty will fall.

— Tu Shih, Hand Infiltrator and Scholar

Out of these warrior kings came the great Qin Shi Huang Di. With a crack of his long whip, Qin drove the universe before him. He conquered the whole of China and proclaimed himself Emperor, the first Emperor since the Divine Sages. His orders became our laws. He developed an expansive bureaucracy, laid out the roads and ordered the collection of taxes. His rule was absolute – his penalties, severe: mutilation, branding, chopping off the hands and feet, castration, strangulation, and decapitation.

He fostered Legalist scholars, who correctly labeled humans as incorrigibly selfish. They found the one road to order – impose laws from above and enforce them severely. These scholars exalted the state, and sought imperial prosperity and martial prowess over the welfare of commoners.

Qin silenced any voices opposed to his rule or Legalism. He exiled or killed thousands of Taoist and Confucian scholars. His soldiers burned any books that challenged his views. He also worked uncountable hoards of laborers to death in several great projects: linking the northern defenses into the Great Wall and constructing the Imperial Palace.

Qin forged an empire that he believed would last ten thousand generations. In truth, it lasted fourteen years. When Qin died, his master of chariots Zhou Gao and his prime minister Li Si concealed his death. They kept Qin's corpse in a heavily-curtained litter and issued proclamations in his name. Arresting all political rivals, or ordering them to commit suicide, they tried to place a beneficial successor on the Dragon Throne. However, after two months of summer heat, they needed to heap a pile of fish beside the imperial litter to disguise the corpse's stench. Suspicion began to grow.

A revolution broke out and Han Kao Tsu, the son of a minor official, rose to power. Han condemned the actions of his predecessor, claiming that Qin was barbaric and cruel. He also reintroduced the Confucian ideal of humane statecraft. Still, Han kept most of Qin's harsh laws, as well as the bureaucracy and the heavy taxation. (This is an important lesson, child. Only strict laws can maintain order – but a sugar coating of empty humanitarian gestures helps everyone swallow it.)

The Han dynasty has ruled for more than two hundred years. We live at the height of Chinese civilization. I have seen the future, and all that follows is a slow decline – a weakening of the Chinese soul. Conquerors will seize the Empire, and it will grow isolated and decadent.

It is our destiny to change that future. Only the strength of the Eaters of the Lotus can maintain this golden age. We must halt the tides of revolution and foreign conquest, for the good of the Empire and our people!

The Land

Our Empire covers a broad range of climates from deserts to tropical rain forests. To help you understand its true breadth, we shall break it into regions.

One primary division is east-west. The west is dry, dominated by deserts, steppes, prairies and mountains. The east is more humid, including the rain forests of the south, the broad-leaved evergreens, bamboo and pine of the central regions, and the taiga-like forests of the extreme north.

Others divide the country north and south. The north is a land of millet, wheat, draft animals and dusty farmlands. The northerners, like yourself, are sturdy, dour, slow, tenacious, straightforward and highly devoted to garlic. The harsh environment has tempered you. Here the rivers bring both life and death. You need the water to irrigate your fields, but the frequent floods can swallow crops or even a village without warning.

The south is a land of rice, lakes, rivers and people who live on the water. Many spend their lives on riverboats as merchants or fishers (often called "lake farmers" by northerners). Southerners, like myself, are often considered quick-tempered, noisy, volatile, devious and given to frivolous pleasures. Devious, yes. The rest I don't know.

Much of the Empire sits on harsh, inhospitable land. The worst environments include the western half of the Tibetan plateau, which is cold, mountainous desert lying above 14,800 feet. Next comes the Loess Plateau, named after the yellow, dusty soil that blows in from the Ordos, Alxa and Gobi deserts. In many places, this dust is hundreds of feet thick. While the yellow soil is fertile, it erodes quickly. The dust also fills the air, accounting for the popularity of spittoons.

Ironically, the capital of Lo-yang lies in the Loess Plateau.

ANIMALS & HUNTING

Domesticated donkeys, camels, yaks, oxen and horses provide mounts and draft animals throughout China — though the best horses come from lands to the east. Yak, sheep and goat provide milk and butter. Wool, though not often used in the Empire, remains important to many living along the northern frontier. Hunters seek out deer, rabbit, pheasant and duck for food. Of the aggressive animals, the most dangerous is the tiger. Many stories describe tigers attacking merchants or traveling ministers — though some believe these "tigers" are really shape-changing humans.

Hunting occupies an important position in the Han culture. The wealthy hunt for entertainment, often stalking quail and deer in safe, controlled parks. Meanwhile, others must hunt for sustenance. Only the adventurous seek out tigers, preferring a prey that fights back.

When hunting, all hunters must make a Perception check to spot their prey. The base difficulty is 5, though you can modify this upwards in particularly-dense terrain or bad lighting. After spotting an animal, the hunters can either flush it (driving it into the open), or shoot it where it stands. The difficulty for hitting hidden prey is 15, or 10 for hitting animals in the open. Resolve the damage as with unnamed characters.

The only exception is the tiger. Tigers come in both named and unnamed varieties, depending on their fierceness. Also, their statistics may vary.

Tiger, unnamed beast

Attributes: Bod 7, Chi 0, Mnd 2, Ref 9
Skills: Intrusion 11, Martial Arts 11
Base Damage: 10 (claws)

Weather

Storms also play an important role in China. Summer monsoons visit the eastern provinces, while great storms annually ravage the southeastern coast. These typhoons cause extensive flooding, especially in the low-lying areas.

Ironically, in the west danger comes from a lack of rain. Droughts cause crops to fail. Snow and freezing temperatures also plague the Tibetan plateau and the extreme north. The rest of the Empire ranges from temperate to tropical weather.

Flora and Fauna

The Empire also boasts a variety of animal life. Northern animals include the Siberian tiger, wolf, badger, lynx, silka deer, musk deer, weasel, sable, stone marten, flying squirrel, snow rabbit, pheasant, mandarin duck and the white-headed crane. The dry western regions host wild donkey, camel, Mongolian gazelle, Mongolian beaver and bighorn sheep. Tibetan antelope, rock sheep, yak, snow leopards and Himalayan brown bears live in the high elevations of Tibet. Meanwhile, the southwest houses the panda, golden cat, clouded leopard, rhesus macaque and goat antelope. Yangtze dolphin, crocodile lizard, golden langur, tiger and various badgers and weasels live in the Yangtze basin. Various monkeys live throughout the south.

Cities

The Empire boasts many large cities. Surrounded by great walls of stone and rammed earth, most have outgrown their allotted space. Poor communities huddle outside these walls — shanty towns filled with the desperate and the damned. (Remember that, child. In the right neighborhoods a few pieces of cash can buy a slit throat or a dagger in the back.) The cities themselves resemble villages — just larger, more sprawling. Their buildings huddle together, and the streets seem more crowded, but few structures reach higher than a single story.

Yet these urban areas act as magnets, gathering scholars and artists. Visit any marketplace and you will see Japanese, Korean, Indian, , Turkish and other Arab merchants. As centers for wealth and trade, our cities have become the most extravagant spots on earth. Still, the vast majority of the population lives in the countryside. Most Chinese are farmers.

City	Population
Ch'eng-tu	282,147
Ch'ang-an	246,200
Lo-yang	195,504
P'eng-ch'eng	148,725

Lo-yang

With the death of Wang Mang the usurper, several factions vied for control over the Empire. The most influential was the Han family, who wished to return to power. Once Guangwu Di (a member of the Han Imperial clan) captured Lo-yang, their return became inevitable. Guangwu crowned himself Emperor. Lo-yang, the center of his power, became his capital.

Over the next ten years, he rebuilt much of Lo-yang according to a strict plan. The heavy walls follow the points of the compass. Three gates open in each of the four walls, each gate flanked by massive watchtowers. Inside, a grid-like pattern of roads divides the city into hundreds of small wards. The City Administrators estimate that 52,839 households rest within the city walls, totaling more than 195,504 individuals. This makes it the third-largest city in the world.

At the main gates in the southern wall, four carts can pass abreast. All the city's major features face south, to collect the flow of positive chi. Even the Dragon Throne in the Imperial Hall faces south.

This city is the center of Chinese culture, and all roads radiate from it. It is also the center of imperial military might. Despite that, Lo-yang sits on the inhospitable Loess

Plateau. Guangwu Di chose to remain here, instead of moving to the more-luxurious south, because it offered easy access to the northern frontiers.

Since its creation, the Empire has faced continual threats from the north and northwest. While the Great Wall offers some protection, the Hsiung-nu continue their raids. Lo-yang's proximity to this volatile region has aided greatly in the Empire's defense.

Unfortunately, the northern provinces cannot support either the Imperial Court or the military. As a result, many trade routes stretch deep into the south and east. Food, supplies and taxes all travel to Lo-yang. The Imperial Bureaucracy skims off their share, then distributes the supplies to the north.

The Imperial Palace

In the center of Lo-yang sprawls the Imperial Palace. Almost a city unto itself, it is a maze of sprawling courtyards, private passageways and pavilions. Tall walls surround it, dotted by narrow towers.

Most of the walls, both inside and out, consist of stone, covered with smooth plaster. Scarlet or white paint finishes the look. The roof boasts half-cylindrical tiles of molded earthware – much better than common thatch.

Only one gate opens to the outside: a heavy archway of gilded stone, sandwiched between two stout towers. Twenty guardsmen, hand-picked from the army, live in these towers. At least two stand guard at all times.

The inside has three main divisions: the outer palace, the pleasure gardens and the inner palace. The outer palace, often called the World of Men, is a narrow ring of courtyards and halls. Here, the Emperor can meet and talk to his advisors, generals and scholars. As with the rest of the palace, the Emperor's eunuchs maintain the World of Men. By tradition, we must protect the Son of Heaven from the baser elements of the outside world. Therefore, his meetings are by strict appointment only.

The World of Men is also the home of the Emperor's male children, once they reach the age of maturity.

The pleasure gardens form a barrier between the World of Men and the inner palace. Men can not enter the pleasure gardens unless invited by the emperor himself. Our guards carefully watch the doorways to both the outer and inner palaces. No one passes through without our knowledge.

The gardens, as you will see, are beautiful. Imperial gardeners boast that they tend a thousand different varieties of trees and a thousand different flowers. Specially-trained merchants import plants from beyond the Empire's borders, and the gardeners then prune them into properly-aesthetic shapes. Here, nothing goes out of season. Silk blooms, silk leaves and delicate perfumes supplement nature when necessary.

A silver lake sits in the gardens' center, the inner palace wrapping around the back half. Brightly-painted boats dot the lake. Smaller lakes and rivers flow throughout both the garden and the inner palace. Most house golden carp.

Scores of exotic animals live within the gardens: monkeys, deer, snow rabbits and even tigers – all docile and tame to the touch. The aviary keeps hundreds of beautiful birds. We even have a delicate butterfly aviary, where special handlers raise and protect the precious insects.

Finally, we have the inner palace. No men can enter here, save the Emperor himself. It is home to five hundred consorts, their maids and the Emperor's eunuchs. We tailor everything to the Emperor's pleasure. Cold rooms for the summer months, with fans and ice to keep the heat at bay. Winter quarters boast fire screens and quilted silk wrappings. Other halls and courtyards are dedicated to the Emperor's whims. These include rooms for music, poetry and philosophy.

In this way, we insure sufficient distractions to keep the Emperor busy and out of the way. Meanwhile, we are free to pursue our own goals. A web of secret passageways, halls and rooms stretches throughout the inner palace. It is the heart of our organization — our private fortress.

Consorts and the Empress

The Son of Heaven keeps more than five hundred consorts, both to prove his superiority to normal men, and more practically, to keep his wives' families from gaining political power. For that reason, imperial advisors (eunuchs, mostly) choose his consorts from poor and middle-class families throughout the Empire. The Son of Heaven picks his favorite to become his Empress, and her eldest son becomes his heir.

However, the desire to keep the consort's families weak does not always succeed. When Emperor Wu Ti died, the widowed Empress Lu tried to seize power. Though she failed to place a family member on the throne, she forged a strong political faction that reached beyond the Imperial Palace. Ninety-five years later, one of her descendants managed to usurp the Dragon Throne — creating the short-lived Xin dynasty.

The current Empress, Jui Szu, was born to a riverboat trader from the far south. As she grew, stories of her beauty spread throughout the province, reaching the ear of its magistrate. Knowing he could gain power by pleasing the Emperor, he took Jui Szu into his household, training her as his own daughter. Her quick mind soon picked up the refined manners of the court, and when she was ready, the magistrate took her to Lo-yang. Within four days of meeting the Emperor, she became one of his consorts.

At that time, another Empress sat on the throne, and Jui Szu was just one among many. For several years, she lived a largely isolated life. She enjoyed some attention from the Emperor, but held a low rank within the hierarchy of women — more a servant than a wife. However, two years after Jui Szu's arrival, the previous Empress died, and the hierarchy of women dissolved.

EMPERORS & NAMES

By tradition, the Son of Heaven's name cannot be spoken, nor can the characters be written. Each Emperor takes a new name when he assumes the throne. The ruling names are typically auspicious, intended to shape the Emperor's reign. The current Emperor chose Harvest of Jade as his ruling name, hoping to bring prosperity to the land.

Upon each emperor's death, the temple grants him a new name. Scholars then use this temple name in all histories written about his reign.

Jui Szu proved remarkably adept at manipulating politics within the inner palace. Using both her beauty and sharp wit, she maneuvered herself into the Emperor's favor. Though less than half his age (or perhaps because of it) she became his favorite — his Empress.

For five years she shared his throne, but she became too crafty — too dangerous. She uncovered our presence and threatened to expose us. We were forced to dispose of her. No, the Emperor would not order her execution — but he cast her from the court. She still performs various ceremonial roles, and, of course, the people love her. But we have pulled the tiger's claws. She is no longer of any concern.

The Emperor

Born in the Xin dynasty, Harvest of Jade was a young man when his father, Guangwu Di, regained the throne. During his youth, he accompanied his father on the campaign trail. He grew into a powerful general in his own right, and continued to lead imperial conquests during Guangwu Di's rule. His military career did not end until he took the throne himself.

However, the ease of palace life quickly corrupted Harvest of Jade. He lost the edge and mental clarity of his youth – preferring to waste his time with women and wine. Now 65 years old, he is more a figurehead than an actual ruler. He approves decisions made by others, often not bothering to read them.

He is a shadow of his former self.

The Government

Why study the government? Once you learn its rules, you can play its games. Yes, child, the government is a game – one we play to win.

Authority passes from Heaven to the Son of Heaven. From him, it trickles down through the bureaucracy. Society is defined by a series of hierarchical relationships and responsibilities. In this way all things are governed.

The government has two major factions: the Central Authority (based in Lo-Yang) and the provincial organs. The Central Authority consults the Emperor and helps him make decisions (or makes decisions in his name – remember that, child). They devise means to collect taxes, and maintain the order and security of the Empire. Below the Emperor, the top-ranking officials are the Prime Minister and the Head of Civil Service. Under these stand the nine major offices of state and the four generals. Which ones have fallen under our sway? Child, some secrets must remain secret.

The Central Authority separates the provinces into commandaries and kingdoms. Currently, the Empire has 83 commandaries and 20 kingdoms. New provinces are added or removed as the Empire expands or retreats across the subcontinent.

The Central Authority assigns a provincial administrator to run the commandaries. Often called Little Emperors, these administrators have relative autonomy. Still, they never serve in their home province, and they must continually move from position to position. This prevents divided loyalties, while limiting the growth of their power base. In fact, few members of the bureaucracy have stable positions for these very reasons. Even in the Central Authority, an official might find himself acquiring tax money for the Office of Agriculture one year, and for the military the next.

We can further divide commandaries into prefectures, districts and finally wards. Each division has its own layer of bureaucracy, often appointed by the provincial authorities.

Meanwhile, the kingdoms are obviously ruled by kings – all near-kinsmen to the Emperor. Theoretically, their hereditary leadership grants them greater autonomy than the commandaries, but in practice, the Central Authority manipulates succession to their advantage. Furthermore, the government in Lo-yang always appoints the king's chief advisor.

All province governments, despite their type, are responsible for collecting the Imperial Tax (in grain, textiles or cash). They must also arrest criminals and keep the peace, draft people for labor or military service, and maintain the Empire's lines of communication.

Eunuchs

Since men cannot enter the inner palace, the Emperor surrounds himself with eunuchs. We maintain the palace, guard the women's quarters, and act as advisors or administrators to the Emperor himself. This guarantees that all offspring borne to the Imperial consorts are descended from the Emperor. (Unless we choose otherwise. Don't laugh, child. Many men would trade their soul for an evening in the inner palace.)

Furthermore, the Emperor believes that all eunuchs are uninterested in collecting wealth and power. Why? Because we told him so. Since we have no offspring, we have no need to build our own dynasties.

Chapter 1

> The eunuchs' belief in their own cleverness would seem humorous, if they were not so dangerous. They waste much of the government's resources in protecting their small pockets of power. Meanwhile, every governor they appoint inevitably buries his provinces under the weight of unending taxation.
>
> Already the peasants mumble complaints about the eunuchs. They know the source of their misfortune. Each day brings them closer to rebellion, but the eunuchs — blinded by their greed — do not see this threat. Eventually, the people will take up swords — stones if necessary. They will find a hero in General He Jin, and the eunuchs will die in the thousands. History has already condemned them.
>
> — *Tu Shih, Hand Infiltrator and Scholar*

In reality, we have little to live for, except the collection of wealth and power.

Most eunuchs are plump. We have little or no facial hair and speak with a high, squeaky voice. Of course, not everyone fits this mold, but those castrated at a younger age tend to conform more closely.

Some of us received castration as a punishment. These often include fallen officials and military officers. Others began as prisoners of war. Most, however, became a eunuch voluntarily. A father can castrate one of his sons, thus ensuring his place in the Imperial Palace. Since the operation is voluntary, it does not threaten family lines. Only a father with many sons would consider it.

Finally, a very few eunuchs castrate themselves. These seek a closeness to the throne – and the political power that comes with it.

Hoi Mao Qian's shoulders burned as he scrubbed the Cloud Hall's tile floor. He had tied his sleeves back, careful not to get them wet. The older eunuchs would punish him for that – or for any number of small offenses.

Five Rats, an older boy whose quarters he shared, oversaw his work today. This meant that Five Rats sat nearby, ready to pounce at the slightest mistake. Five Rats seemed to enjoy the punishments. He sought out excuses. If not during their chores, then later when they were alone.

Mao Qian had spent nearly four hours scrubbing and rescrubbing the room. He had hauled in six buckets of clean water, and hauled out five of dirty. Dipping the brush in the bucket one last time, he finished the final corner, then rocked back, sitting on his ankles.

"You've stopped." Five Rats was at his side, before he had a chance to catch his breath.

"Yes." Mao Qian bowed his head, "This humble servant has finished the task set for him."

"Finished?" Five Rats laughed. "You can't be finished. This place is still filthy."

Mao Qian looked around. Every inch of the floor seemed to sparkle. "This humble servant apologizes. If you could but show me a spot of dirt, I will gladly scrub it away."

Five Rats smiled. "Then look over here." He walked out into the center of the room, hitched up his robe and defecated on the floor. "Just look at this mess. If you missed this, who knows what other mistakes you've made. Clean it up, then scrub the floor again – the whole floor."

Mao could feel the fire of anger growing within his belly, but he knew better than to respond. Five Rats' eyes twinkled as he fingered the bamboo lash tucked under his sash. He wanted Mao to complain – wanted an excuse to whip him.

Mao clenched his jaw and nodded. Picking up both brush and bucket, he walked slowly to the center of the room. As he crouched beside the pile of filth, Mao's hand fell on his shoulder, squeezing it tightly.

"No, no. That water is too dirty. Go empty it and fetch new."

"Yes, sir." Mao stood slowly, lifting the bucket by its rough rope handle.

"And don't take too long. We've got another room to scrub once we're done here."

Muttering curses under his breath, Mao trudged out into the hallway. The nearest stream was just two rooms away, but he had to empty the bucket first. That meant walking to the Filth Room – a ten-minute trek.

By now his body automatically navigated the winding passages of the Inner Palace. Many men would kill to get in here. Mao would kill to get out. He had considered it often – when Five Rats and the others were asleep. He could strangle them one by one. His head would surely decorate the palace wall by morning, but it might just be worth it.

As he rounded the next corner, a movement caught his eye. Stopping, Mao watched as part of the wall settled back into place.

Odd, he thought. Setting down the bucket and brush, he approached the wall. It seemed solid enough, but as he tapped it with one knuckle, the drum-like sound gave it away. A secret passageway, The other boys had spoken of such things. But how did it open? Should he even try?

Mao shook his head and leaned against it. It refused to budge. Looking closer, he spotted the hair-fine crack running around the edge of the door, then noticed a nearby floor tile a touch taller than the rest. As he stepped on the tile, a faint groan echoed from the wall, and the panel slid open.

Thick incense spilled out into the hallway. Inside, the room seemed to dance with the light from a thousand candles. An old man sat in the center, his legs folded into the lotus position, open hands resting on his knees.

Mao hurried to close the door, but just then the old man's eyes snapped open. "Ah, Hoi Mao Qian." He said, in a ridiculously high voice. "Come in, I have been expecting you."

Mao took a tentative step forward. "Expecting me?"

"Yes. We have much to discuss, you and I. You have delayed too long already."

Mao's glanced back at his bucket. "But – "

"Leave it. Five Rats can clean up his own filth. He is thickheaded – not good for anything but hard work and breaking bones. You, however, have real promise. Have you ever heard of the Eaters of the Lotus?"

"Lotus Eaters?" Mao asked.

"No, child. Eaters of the Lotus. Magic and true power. Sit. We have much to discuss..."

CHAPTER 2

History of the Lotus

For the benefit of those new to our order, I have put brush to ink. This history, humbly written, offers a sense of continuity and a connection to the past. Read it and learn of our greatness.

It began when I, Gao Zhang, ascended to the governorship of the Chen-wei province more than forty years ago. Chen-wei is a cold land, filled with bitter, lawless people. Though I struggled tirelessly to bring order to the region, they would have none of it. They turned to open rebellion, in defiance of myself and the Emperor.

Impudent fools! I set my troops against them, and for several months we slaughtered the rabble. Many villages burned brightly, lighting up the night sky. Then, just as their resolve began to crumble, my incompetent captain led his forces into a rebel trap. Hidden crossbowmen cut the army down. They returned his head in a silk-lined box.

Word of this defeat quickly reached the Emperor's ears, magnified by those in league with the rebels. The old fool was too doddered to recognize the truth, and ordered my return to Lo-yang. Doing so, he pulled the remaining pillar of law from under the region, and it collapsed into chaos. Then, he dared blame me for the disaster.

He accused me of treason and condemned me to castration. For nearly two years, I served as his personal assistant. My greatness was reduced to fetching embroidered robes and wine.

But I refused to lose hope. Lying alone in my cramped quarters, my mind conceived of an elaborate plan. I served the Emperor dutifully, never showing my true revulsion. I studied the workings of the court, learned its secrets and the secrets to power. Soon, my efforts paid off. The Emperor began to trust me. I acted as his scribe, writing and delivering both personal messages and imperial edicts.

That is the first lesson: information carries its own power. By changing a few words, or delaying an important message, I began to influence the shape of the Empire. I siphoned off a measure of wealth and power.

Other eunuchs recognized my strength and began to flock to my side. We blocked all access to the Emperor, refusing audiences unless properly bribed. If anyone opposed us, we cut them off entirely. Eventually, we hired bandits or gangs of armed thugs to enforce our will.

Still, none of this is new. It had been done before, and better, by others. My true rise began with the arrest of three outlaws.

The Ten Thousand Eyes

Yin Shu, Er Chan and Gui Long belonged to an occult secret society, named the Ten Thousand Eyes. Founded during the early Zhou dynasty, the Ten Thousand Eyes once

Gao Zhang, Center of the Lotus

Attributes: Bod 7, Chi 0 (For 4, Mag 14), Mnd 9, Ref 7
Skills: Deceit 15, Detection 12, Info/Demons 15, Info/Imperial Bureaucracy 14, Info/Imperial China 12, Leadership 14, Sorcery 22
Schticks: Blast (all), Divination, Fertility, Healing, Influence, Movement, Summoning.
Base Damage: 16 (blast)

had informants stationed in every minor court throughout the subcontinent. They cast great spells, causing rivers to flood or wrapping the land in drought. Their magic shortened the lives of many kings and extended the reigns of others.

At first, they were not interested in matters of money or power. They acted as spiritual guides, forging the land into an empire to rival the Jade Emperor's. With an unseen hand, they directed the fate of thousands, trying to build a golden future. They understood how hardship could strengthen an individual — how destruction could clear the path for new growth. These became their tools.

However, they did not understand the corruption inherent in all humans. As time passed, the lure of wealth and power tempted many Eyes. A few began to accept bribes, promising supernatural aid in return. This went undetected for decades.

Eventually, however, the inner council noticed and decided to move against their wayward members. But those who had gathered wealth and political favors did not hesitate to use their newfound influence against their old masters. The infighting grew fierce as the society's foundation fragmented. Hundreds of the Eyes died or faced arrest. Others continued to grow fat off the payments from their patrons.

Greed spread and eventually the Eyes hungered for more than just material wealth. They turned to the Underworld, offering the demons their services in exchange for supernatural assistance. The demons readily agreed, seeing an opportunity for corruption and power

The Ten Thousand Eyes continued their slide into decadence. Demons encouraged various cells to quarrel, promoting paranoia and often outright violence. Centuries passed, and the once-great order withered and died. The infernal pact was meant to increase their power, but it actually reduced it as they faded into a mere shadow of their previous glory.

When Qin Shi Huang Di united the Empire, the Ten Thousand Eyes were too weak to stand against him. Qin burned more than just the books of scholars. Sorcerers also earned his wrath. He executed any he could find, their tomes fed to the flames.

By the time I met Yin Shu, Er Chan and Gui Long, the Eyes were only a handful of sorcerers huddled together in Lo-yang. Similar cells survived in Ch'ang-an, P'eng-ch'eng and Hsai-p'ei.

I was born in Chen-wei. It is a dry, harsh land. Little grows in its rocky soil — but that did not keep Gao Zhang from extracting his taxes.

He ruled the province like an Emperor. There was no appeal higher than his word, and the imperial troops carried out his wishes with brutal efficiency. But even his orders could not make the grain grow.

My people gave everything to Gao's tax collectors. We starved ourselves, but still he wanted more. In the end, we had no choice but revolution. At first it went badly. The imperial troops slaughtered us whenever they found us. When they couldn't, they burned our villages to the ground. But Gao's excesses weighed heavily on the region. Our numbers swelled as the revolution spread throughout the province and beyond. We began to face the imperials on an even footing — and then we began to win.

— *Bandit Lord Spearbreaker*

Initiation

Within the imperial palace, I had expanded my influence as far as I dared. Already, several bureaucrats complained about my manipulations. If their words reached the Emperor, my life would be forfeit.

Then I heard about Yin Shu, Er Chan and Gui Long. A gate guard spotted them entering the city with a wagon of partially-decomposed corpses. When he tried to stop them, they began tossing about balls of flaming ash and acid. Eventually, guards captured the sorcerers, but not before they accidentally set fire to several wards.

More than twenty people died in the battle. I knew that the military would insist on an execution. Still, the sorcerers represented a source of untapped power. I had the palace guards bring them to me. In a remote corner of the outer palace, I interviewed them, and finally promised to spare their lives if they taught me the dark arts.

The sorcerers hesitantly agreed. They drew a bowl of my own blood and painted the eight trigrams on my body. Then sharing a drink of rice wine, they initiated me into the Ten Thousand Eyes.

I ordered my men to capture and bathe three beggars. Dressing them in the sorcerers' robes, I ordered their execution. Meanwhile, I arranged permanent quarters for Yin Shu and the others.

As fate would have it, I had a natural talent for sorcery. I also realized that Yin Shu and his companions were short-sighted and weak. They taught me a lot, but in the end, they were slaves to their powers — not masters. Within two years, I had absorbed all they could teach me. This learning went beyond magic. The collapse of the Ten Thousand Eyes revealed much about my own failures.

Armed with this new knowledge, I decided to expand my power base. As a first step, I disposed of my mentors, then destroyed the remaining Eyes within Lo-yang. Next, I chose eight loyal eunuchs. Together we formed the inner circle of a new secret society — the Eaters of the Lotus. I became the Center of the Lotus. They became the Petals.

Gao Zhang Seizes Power

I moved to ensure the loyalty of all eunuchs in the palace. The trustworthy joined the Eaters of the Lotus. Others I employed as mooks and leg-breakers. Step by step, we removed any threats. The squeamish quickly fell victim to unfortunate accidents, found themselves convicted of various crimes, or simply vanished.

Next I began arranging appointments and promotions to loyal scholars and officials. Armed thugs harassed anyone who rose against our will. If that did not work, I gathered the Petals, and we summoned a host of demons and ghosts to handle the problem.

Slowly we spread tendrils of power out from Lo-yang. Our sorcerers began to roam the Empire, infesting the countryside with demons and hungry spirits. After letting their fiends ravage for a week, the sorcerer would then arrive in town, offering to exorcise the creatures for a healthy fee. If the villagers hesitated, the infernal attacks became more violent, and the price went up. Eventually they all agreed. The sorcerers reigned in their spirits, sending them farther down the road. In this way, we gathered money and demanded obedience.

As our power grew, so did the need for caution. I began conducting more business through successive levels of henchmen. Each had only a slim view of the overall picture, and none knew about the Lotus. Whenever an inquisitive courtier came too close, I created a scapegoat to accept the blame.

I also employed the skills of feng shui professors. We asked the Emperor to build sev-

Hu Lei, sorcerer of the Ten Thousand Eyes

Attributes: Bod 5, Chi 0 (Mag 8), Mnd 6, Ref 5
Skills: Deceit 8, Infiltration 12, Sorcery 17
Schticks: Divination, Influence, Movement, Summoning
Notes: Hu Lei watched Gao Zhang's henchmen destroy his cell in Lo-yang. He escaped — barely — and hid. Twenty men died. As the years passed, he planned his vengeance. He gathered his demonic servants, and listened to their whispering. He has followed the rise of Gao Zhang and his eunuchs, and soon he hopes to take vengeance against the Center of the Lotus.

eral towers throughout Lo-yang. Since the Gods prefer towering structures, I easily convinced him that they would help win divine favor. Imperial scribes could also use them to observe the heavens or chart the chi flow. In truth, they became feng shui sites — to which the Lotus became attuned.

The greatest of these is the Hall of Brilliance. Built within the Imperial Pleasure Gardens, the hall ensured the continuing prosperity of the Han dynasty. Though its proposal raised a controversy among the court scholars, I convinced the Emperor of its benefits. As with all these constructs, I offered to staff and maintain it with eunuchs — thus giving us control over its chi.

However, the Hall of Brilliance differed from other minor feng shui sites — it fed from the chi of Lo-yang. The south-facing gates drew chi from the surrounding countryside, indeed from the entire Empire. Likewise, the imperial palace absorbed chi from throughout the city. The Hall of Brilliance became the final basin for all of this — focusing it into one spot.

Lotus Membership

When Gao Zhang created the Eaters of the Lotus, it was little more than a loosely-knit group of confidants and strongmen. Gao was the leader. Everyone else followed his orders. No one needed further organization.

However, Gao had a vision. He wanted more than a group of conspirators gathering in unused halls. He wanted power, and true power demands a rigid hierarchy.

(**Note:** this hierarchy only applies to people initiated into the Eaters of the Lotus. The Lotus traditionally use a large number of outsiders — hired thugs, freelance sorcerers, demons and such. Few of these know the truth behind their masters. Hired or summoned by individuals, they serve that individual. Those who know about the Lotus keep that information to themselves.)

For the most part, outsiders are the absolute lowest rank. They are unworthy of initiation into the Lotus. Some, however, deserve recognition. These include powerful beings who either are ineligible for membership or have refused it. Demons, females, influential mercenaries and hermits all fall into this category. However, because of their abilities and their service to the Lotus, they often command obedience from moderate (and sometimes even high) ranking members.

Ironically, a growing number of demons have begun demanding obedience, instead of meekly offering their services. Several Petals have become worried by this trend. Even Gao recognizes it as a potential problem — after all, he knows how the demons wrecked the Ten Thousand Eyes. However, he believes that any sorcerer who summons a spirit he cannot control deserves whatever he gets.

Hierarchy

Gao is the Center of the Lotus, the faction's undisputed leader. While he has established specific and exacting rules governing replacements for every other rank, Gao has not set any guidelines for choosing his own replacement. While this may seem like a ploy to keep others from coveting his position, in truth Gao has no intention of retiring or dying. This has led many people to believe

Plague Bearer, demonic punisher

Attributes: Body 5 (Tgh 10), Chi 0 (Mag 4), Mnd 4, Ref 4
Skills: Creature Power 18
Schticks: Blast (disease), Insubstantial (cannot pass through wood)
Unique Schtick
Contagious Attack: Anyone touching a character infected with Plague Bearer's Blast (disease) must roll a Con check (difficulty 10) or also become infected. Treat this as a new attack.
Notes: During the early days of the Lotus, one of Gao's priests summoned the Plague Bearer to harass a small, southern community. Unfortunately, Plague Bearer proved too good at his job. His disease spread unchecked through the village. Within a month, everyone was dead. Gao has since kept track of Plague Bearer — carefully using his talents to destroy or incapacitate problem cities, villages, fortresses and clans.

that they will only replace Gao by killing him. So far, no one wants to try.

Next, under Gao, are the Petals of the Lotus. The Petals act as a ruling council. They organize the long-range plans for the Eaters of the Lotus, distribute resources and approve awards of rank and honor.

They consist of eight members each named after one of the eight trigrams. However, these are not the trigrams recorded in the I Ching. Rather, they are dark reflections. The reverse trigrams include The Underworld, Emptiness, Silence, Drought, The Pit, Stillness, Frost, and Desert. All the Petals are eunuchs – originally the first eight that Gao inducted. However, Gao has since replaced all but two of the original members.

Sorcerous ability is almost a prerequisite for holding a seat among the Petals. However, Shi Zi Hui, the current Desert, cannot cast even the smallest spells – his strategic thinking and battlefield prowess earned his seat.

Shi Zi Hui used to be the Imperial General in charge of the Northern Frontier. Then he lost a decisive battle against the Hsiung-nu. They took him prisoner, dragging him north into their lands. Meanwhile, they continued to raid deep into the Empire.

Shi remained with the Hsiung-nu for more than five years. At first he was little more than a slave – but his fighting prowess soon impressed them. They let Shi ride on raids against other clans, soon letting him lead his own. During one of these, Shi broke ranks and escaped back across the Northern Frontier.

Unfortunately, imperial troops spotted and captured him. Though the men once served under Shi, they believed he was a traitor. A long-standing imperial edict condemned him – so they followed its orders, castrating him on the spot, then shipping him back to Lo-yang.

He served in the Imperial Palace for less than a week before catching Gao's attention. Like the Hsiung-nu, Gao recognized Shi's impressive knowledge of warcraft. Since that day, he has helped plan all major offensives.

Though all the Petals are theoretically the same rank, a rough seniority has developed among them. The Underworld is the top; Desert is the bottom.

Oddly, after accepting their seat, each petal soon manifests various aspects from their trigram. Some believe this is a spiritual side effect, somehow forged during their initiation to the seat. Others claim it is simply an affectation.

Thorns & Vassals

Gao has divided the remaining membership among two ranks – the Thorns of the Lotus and the Vassals of the Lotus. He expects the Thorns to operate without direct supervision, trusting them to execute orders and act upon their own initiative. Vassals, on the other hand, always serve under the watchful eye of a Thorn. They are simple mooks, not expected (or allowed) to think for themselves.

Gao has often considered expanding this system, to include several layers of fine dis-

Shi Zi Hui, Petal of the Desert

Attributes: Bod 7 (Tgh 9), Chi 0, Mnd 6 (Cha 8), Ref 7
Skills: Info/Military Logistics 14, Info/Tactics 15, Martial Arts 19
Unique Schticks
Leads by Example: All Lotus mooks gain + 1 AV while fighting with Shi Zi Hui. Only affects troops in his immediate vicinity.
Base Damage: 11 (sword)
Notes: Shi Zi Hui both controls palace security and organizes all Lotus expansionary forces. When a battle really matters, he goes out and leads the troops personally.

tinction. Instead, demonic advice led him to add layers of titles and honors atop these ranks.

Titles describe the actual responsibility each person commands. Typical titles include General (military command of an entire region or juncture), Captain (controls a small force), Lieutenant (second in command) and Administrator (logistical commander). Some get quite specific — Assistant to the Administrator, Overseeing Field Reports.

Titled members are theoretically in charge of everything under their auspices. No one except Gao and the Petals can question their word. However, many titles overlap, causing some confusion.

Honors, on the other hand, include uncountable badges, awards and ceremonial offices. None of these command real power — which is why they appealed to Gao. He can hand them out liberally, limited only by his imagination.

Typical honors include the Blood of the Loyal (given to those injured in battle) and the Mark of the Lotus (a high honor awarded by the Petals). Officers can also give out the Jade Leaf as a mark of debt. The owner can redeem it anytime — though most choose to collect them, hoping the officer will increase in rank, and thus in power. A few honors are very obscure. The Master of the Pool of Blood is a prime example. As far as anyone knows, there is no actual pool of blood. Still, major rituals require the Master's presence.

Gao has further separated the ranks into five divisions, named after the elements: Water, Fire, Metal, Wood and Earth. The Water division encompasses the Lotus's bureaucracy. It is the backbone. The Water maintains supplies, collects and distributes resources, and organizes training. It maintains the lines of communication. While this seems unglamorous, the Water also includes the Petals and most high-titled Thorns. It also incorporates the Pillars of Heaven — one of Gao's internal policing organizations.

The Metal division handles all Lotus research. This was originally limited to a small group of sorcerous experimenters and fortune tellers. However, since the discovery of the Netherworld, this division has nearly quadrupled. It now includes exploration of the Netherworld, other Junctures and future history.

The Wood division handles all spies — even those that keep an eye on Lotus activities. According to Master Sun Tzu, there are five types of spies: the local spy, the inside spy, the reverse spy, the dead spy and the living spy. You hire local spies from the region's indigenous population. Inside spies come from the disaffected ranks of the enemy. These include relatives of executed criminals, officials wrongfully punished or passed up for promotion, and those whose greed exceeds their loyalty. Reverse spies are enemy infiltrators whose temporary loyalty you purchase. While they may continue to work for the enemy, they also give you information. These include double agents and renegades.

Dead spies generally include incompetent spies sent into enemy territory with false information. You know that the enemy will capture them and gain all the information they carry. The enemy will then make plans accordingly — killing the spies once they realize their betrayal.

Note: When you feed enemy spies disinformation, they become dead spies. This accomplishes two goals. It misleads the enemy, while ridding you of a potentially dangerous infiltrator.

Living spies are necessarily the most trusted. They pass back and forth through enemy territory, gathering information and communicating with local infiltrators. Because of this, you must choose them carefully. They should appear inconspicuous, perhaps even stupid, but the job requires an inner strength. They must be fast, powerful, brave and immune to seduction. They need to willingly face cold, heat, hunger, thirst, pain and dishonor.

However, since Gao trusts no one, he binds all of the Lotus's living spies with magic. Perhaps their head explodes with a blast of fire. Perhaps they become gibbering idiots. In any case, no one betrays the Eaters of the Lotus.

While the Wood roster includes all five varieties, they also keep an eye on the Empire and on Lotus activities. One of the Wood's largest subdivisions is the Silent Eyes — the Lotus's internal police.

The Fire division handles the Lotus's expansion forces. These are typically small teams with a specific specialization. They range from mobs of hired thugs and recruitment teams to supernatural terrorists, strike forces and trouble-shooters. This is one of the most glamorous divisions. Anyone assigned to the Fire division quickly gains honors, ranks and titles. If a person does not want to study magic or become a eunuch, this is often their only chance to gain prestige — provided they survive. The Fire division has the highest casualty rates of any Lotus division (even higher than casualties among the hired help).

The final division is the Earth. While technically the Lotus's defense, it includes all standing military forces. For the most part, they organize the Lotus's infiltration into the imperial army, but it also includes groups of bandits and private warriors hired by the Lotus. Unlike the Fire division, the Earth forces consist of groups meant for mass combat.

During her rebellion, Empress Lu created the Order of the Empress — a secret alliance that included both magistrates and revolutionary scholars. They sought to reform the excesses of the Han dynasty by placing one of Lu's family on the Dragon Throne.

Despite Empress Lu's defeat, the Order of the Empress continued to grow. Eventually, they assisted Wang Mang's bid for power, and formed the short-lived Xin dynasty. When the Han dynasty returned to power, the resulting persecution decimated their numbers.

The survivors flocked to Empress Jui Szu upon her exile. She has since rebuilt the order into a strong political and military force.

— Dr. John Haynes, Dragon Observer, Full-Contact Historian and High-Caliber Anthropologist

When referring to a person, Lotus members typically use both the division and rank. For example, Bing Hi, the Lotus in charge of Lo-yang's iron stores, is a Water Vassal. On the other hand, Fei Sheng — the leader of an elite troubleshooting team — is a Fire Thorn. Sometimes titles and honors are also added.

This dizzying mix of ranks, honors, titles and divisions makes it difficult to tell exactly who is superior to whom (which is probably why the demons recommended it). It lends itself to interpretation and confusion. In the end, every member has as much respect and power as they can seize and hold.

The Lotus & the Empire

In many ways, the Eaters of the Lotus are a parasite, feeding off the Empire's strength. Yes, they have their own armies and hired mooks. Yes, they can summon demons, ghosts and spirits to torment their enemies — but their true power lies in their ability to influence the Emperor.

Through the Emperor they gain indirect control over the imperial army and all officers of the bureaucracy. The Lotus can access the Empire's resources. They can create laws and issue imperial edicts.

Consequently, the Eaters of the Lotus are strongest where the Empire is strong. Their power focuses on the cities, especially Lo-yang, Ch'ang-an and P'eng-ch'eng. In the countryside their influence lessens, depending on the loyalty and reliability of their on-site members. Usually one Lotus will control a large area. This spreading becomes worse as you move into the fringes of the Empire. In some places, a single Thorn watches over an entire province.

Also, the Lotus have little influence on the sovereign kingdoms that exist within the Empire, or in any of the lands outside the Empire's borders. Gao Zhang has sent some teams to infiltrate these lands — especially the Hsiung-nu and the imperial kingdoms. Lotus explorers even reached the edge of Rome. However, while they may pave the way for later influence, they offer little immediate control.

Command Centers

To try and bring some order to their operations, the Lotus established command centers throughout the Empire and beyond. These centers act as gathering points for information, and depots for supplies. The Lotus almost always place them on strong feng shui sites.

In many ways, these command centers look like duplicates of the provincial magistrates' palaces. A single Lotus member from the Water division runs the center and all lands under its command. He typically controls a company from the Earth division and perhaps a Fire squad or two — though some centers have only a handful of mooks.

Every command center will try to further the Lotus goals within their region. Unfortunately, in the extreme frontiers, they often become mere guards. They keep an eye

It is true that few magistrates dare oppose Gao Zhang openly. Still, few support him willingly. The case of Wen Zi, however, is interesting. Wen moved to stop Gao's emergency taxation — not because he cared for the welfare of his people, but because it cut into his own income. The people of the Shu province already suffered under heavy taxes — anything that Gao took from them came directly from Wen's coffers.

Wen's further willingness to stand against the forces of the Empire made him a hero of the people. Not that he had any choice — his head was already forfeit. Still, he promised them broad cuts in taxes in return for their aid. Many simple farmers joined him at the provincial palace — joined him and died.

— *Tu Shih, Hand Infiltrator and Scholar*

Empress Jui Szu

Attributes: Bod 5, Chi 0 (For 6), Mnd 7 (Cha 10), Ref 6

Skills: Guns 13, Info/Imperial Bureaucracy 13, Info/Imperial China 13, Info/Rebels 10, Leadership 14, Martial Arts 10

Notes: Empress Jui Szu now lives in a small imperial temple in the back of Lo-yang. Her continued activities in the capital have attracted some unhealthy attention. The Order of the Empress has already stopped two attacks on her life. Since then, several of Jui Szu's more-militant friends have begun training her to defend herself. She already knew how to use a bow — though she had only used it for target practice. She also keeps a dozen Order of the Empress henchmen around her, just in case.

Order of the Empress, loyal henchmen

Attributes: Bod 6, Chi 0, Mnd 5, Ref 6

Skills: Detective 12, Gun 10, Martial Arts 13

Base Damage: 10 (sword), 7 (bow)

out for rebellion, questionable activities, and other factions, then report these to the Petals.

The Petals then organize an official response – usually by sending Fire teams or Earth companies into the region. Remember: the areas closest to Lo-yang and the other major cities have priority. When disasters strike multiple places at once (for instance, after the Jammers destroy an important feng shui site), the Petals may instruct their remote members to "Handle the problem to the best of your abilities and wait for further instructions."

Empress Jui Szu

Even with the new fortune gained by these sites, not all went well for the Eaters of the Lotus. Empress Jui Szu began to grow suspicious. She and her ladies heard the rumors drifting around the palace. They noticed strange meetings and suspicious gatherings. They found once-open halls now locked and guarded.

Empress Jui Szu presented these fears to her husband. And soon, the Emperor began looking at me with a suspicious glare. My power base began to unravel, as minor eunuchs abandoned my service in search of more secure patrons. Even a few sorcerers turned from me. Poor fools – they learned too late their folly, and paid for their lack of faith.

Still, I needed to act if I wanted to keep my head. My loyal servants created evidence of a false sorcerous society within the imperial palace. I then brought this before the Emperor. Those who turned against me found themselves accused of consorting with demons and conspiring against the throne. Then I abased myself before the Son of Heaven, saying that, though I knew nothing of my underling's treachery, I would share the blame for their actions.

The Emperor, moved by my play of humble servitude, spared my life while executing those I exposed. In return, I promised to continue my investigations, until they came to the root of the problem. Not surprisingly, that root was Empress Jui Szu and her eldest son.

Harvest of Jade ordered the boy to commit suicide, but could not execute his favorite wife. Instead, he exiled her from the palace, and stripped her of all power.

With that, the danger passed. Still, I worried that our simple-minded Emperor might turn against me one day. To prevent any further problems, I summoned a demon of nightmares, ordering it to visit the Son of Heaven every night for a week.

Each night when he cried out, I arrived with a sleeping draught in hand. As he drained the potion, I reigned in the demon. He slept the rest of the night in peace. As I expected, Harvest of Jade quickly became dependent on the draught (which was just spiced rice wine). From that day on, whenever he questioned my actions or authority, I threatened to withhold the draught. All objections or arguments stammered to a close, as fear of the nightmares washed over him.

The Secret War

For the next twenty-five years, I concentrated my efforts on the Empire. Once we secured a power base in Lo-yang, I moved to bring other provinces under my control. Then, we expanded into the imperial colonies in Korea and Vietnam, while fortifying the Empire's northern border.

Caution was still necessary in the imperial palace. I drove the affairs of state through subtle manipulations and sorcerous might. However, in the remote provinces our actions were more free.

My private army marched over the subcontinent. Under the guise of emergency taxation, they raided villages. My bandits and armed thugs greeted all protests with violence: executing their leaders, then burning both towns and crops to the ground. Lotus sorcerers also flooded trouble spots with demons and ghosts. In extreme cases, we called on support from the imperial army itself.

Few magistrates dared oppose me.

However, in the Shu province along the far western frontier lived a treacherous man, the magistrate Wen Zi. I must credit Wen for his bravery, though not for his wisdom. He ordered Shu's imperial troops to capture the Lotus henchmen in the region.

My response was swift and decisive. I arranged an imperial edict for Wen Zi's arrest, sentencing him to death by decapitation. Other edicts commanded the local troops to stand down. Any who refused would share Wen Zi's punishment.

Commander An Bao led new troops in to secure the region. I sent along a small cadre of sorcerers, insuring a plague of spirits to punish those who escaped the imperial law.

Most of Wen Zi's troops abandoned him. The remaining barricaded themselves in the provincial palace. The fortress walls proved sufficient to hold off our mortal troops — but not our supernatural ones. When An Bao finally broke through the palace's outer wall, he found everyone inside dead. The corpses showed no obvious signs of injury — but they lay like half-drained wineskins, not a single bone remaining inside their bodies.

Still, some rebels managed to retreat into the mountains. An Bao and the sorcerers continued their pacification of the region; however, his soldiers began reporting heavy losses, particularly when accompanied by supernatural creatures. They described encounters with highly-trained units, dressed in outlandish clothing and carrying odd objects. These objects seemed to focus magical energy, as they cast blasts of fire, bolts of blue lightning, and waves of pure agony.

These soldiers attacked the imperial troops and outlaws alike, though they largely focused their fire on the demons, ghosts and spirits present. Once they immobilized the supernat-

Bone Drinker, minor demonic infiltrator

Attributes: Body 4 (Tgh 8), Chi 0, (Mag 8), Mnd 5, Ref 7
Skills: Creature Power 16, Deceit 12, Intimidation 12, Intrusion 12, Martial Arts 14
Schticks: Blast (Transmutation), Blindspot, Voice Mimicry
Base Damage: 18 (blast), 5 (claws)
Notes: Bone Drinker uses his blast attack to transmute his targets' bones to jelly. Once he incapacitates his victims, he feeds off their liquefied skeleton.

The Lotus frequently hire Bone Drinker to infiltrate opposing strongholds. He easily slips past most barriers, going directly for the stronghold's leadership. After feeding on these, he begins decimating the troops. This often drives the fear-crazed survivors directly into the Lotus's waiting army.

ural creatures, they would seize them and retreat.

An Bao decided to focus his resources on this new threat, but found that they fought as well as his best warriors. Skirmishes continued for many months. He won several battles, but never seemed to gain any true victories. This enemy did not care about capturing or holding territory. They did not have any supply lines or fortresses. When they retreated from battle, they disappeared completely.

Eventually, a young swordsman named Meng Jen led a small force of archers and walking corpses on a patrol through the Shu mountains. There, they fell into an outlander ambush. A glob of blue ectoplasm splashed over his troops, and the corpses froze in mid-step. Explosions ripped through Meng Jen's men. The rest broke ranks and fled.

Meng Jen was the only one to stay behind. A blast knocked him down, where he froze, paralyzed by fear. Lying among the dead, he watched as the strangers clambered from their hiding places and clasp shining, silver manacles on the walking corpses. Soon, the corpses started moving again, and the outlanders prodded them deeper into the mountains.

Embarrassed by his show of weakness, Meng Jen decided to win back his honor. He crept along behind the strangers, watching them carefully. After an hour's hike, they arrived at a sheer cliff. A narrow trail led down to the dark mouth of a cave. The strangers marched straight into the cave, not bothering to leave a sentry outside.

Meng Jen waited for a while, then slipped down to the cave mouth and listened. But instead of hearing voices, he heard a faint howling, like a fall wind whistling over a chimney. Cautiously, he took a few steps inside.

The yellowish-tan rock walls soon lost their color, turning a flat gray. The air grew stuffy and hot. It seemed thick with a dust that stuck to Meng Jen's tongue. Twisted passageways led off in several directions, each lit by an eerie, sourceless light. Meng Jen reached out to touch the wall, it felt warm and slippery under his fingers.

Trying to find the strangers, Meng Jen carefully picked his way along the tunnels, but they seemed to shift behind his back. Within minutes, he was hopelessly lost. He searched frantically for the way out. Time seemed to stretch as he wandered among the featureless caverns.

After what seemed like weeks, he stumbled through a small opening, and found himself lying at the base of a giant willow. Two days later, he arrived at the provincial palace.

He reported the incident to An Bao, but the commander did not believe the story. An Bao accused Meng Jen of desertion. He stripped the lieutenant of all rank, and chopped off his left hand as punishment. Meng Jen became little more than a slave, hauling and stacking supplies in the provincial compound.

But other reports began filtering in. More imperial soldiers spotted the strange enemy disappearing into caves, behind waterfalls and into the trunks of trees. These rumors soon reached my ears in Lo-yang.

I issued an imperial decree that pardoned Meng Jen of all crimes, returning his rank and honor. Furthermore I chose him to co-lead an expedition into this new realm. He was partnered with the eunuch sorcerer Shen Yo.

Equipped with two hundred swordsmen and archers, ghost, demons, spirits and supplies for two months, the two entered Meng Jen's cave. They soon came upon crude houses and lone rabble living along the maze of passageways. From these, they learned about the Netherworld: the Inner Kingdom, gateways, and even the secret war.

They stepped out into the 1850 and Contemporary juncture, grabbing various treasures as evidence of their journey. They also explored the Inner Kingdom, trading food for many strange and wondrous devices. Many of these dissolved as soon as they exited the Netherworld, but enough survived. Their journey forever changed our view of the world — and our goals.

Since that time the Eaters of the Lotus have emphasized further exploration of Netherworld and other junctures. I have learned of other groups seeking to control not only their home Juncture, but all time. The Order of the Wheel, Jade Wheel Society, the Buro and the Guiding Hand — these have become our enemies. My spies have studied Chinese history, learning of our eventual downfall — a downfall I intend to avoid. Covert Lotus groups now operate in every juncture, and soon we will spread our Empire through all time.

Meanwhile, Meng Jen left the imperial army to create an elite strike force of Netherworld Rabble. Meng Jen still serves the Lotus as a mercenary — though his loyalties are suspect. He has a growing fondness for the 1990s juncture, and has open ties with both the Dragons and the Four Monarchs.

Shen Yo continues to explore the Netherworld. His primary mission includes

Meng Jen

Attributes: Bod 8, Chi 4 (for 5), Mnd 6, Ref 7
Skills: Guns 12, Info/Lotus 10, Info/Netherworld 8, Martial Arts 18
Schticks: Loyal Steel, Flying Sword
Unique Schtick
Friend of Steel: Meng Jen has +2 armor against blade weapons. Any sword acts as a signature weapon in his hands.
Base Damage: 12 (sword), 7 (bow)

gathering information on the Netherworld and the Lotus's enemies there; however, he has also began studying the art of shaping, and examines the usefulness of permanent strongholds within the Netherworld. His reports on Guiyu Zui, the gateway to the underworld, are fascinating, and he frequently uses that palace as a staging area.

Future History

When my spies returned from the future, I was surprised to learn that so-called reformers would destroy the Lotus within 60 years. In 129 A.D. an imperial general named Han Jin rose to power on a wave of popular discontent. He stormed the imperial palace, killing the Emperor, shattering the Han dynasty and murdering palace eunuchs by the thousands. The Eaters of the Lotus tried to strike back, but Han's army hunted them down. I must assume that no one survived, for no amount of searching has uncovered any further traces of our influence.

Shocked by the news, I had the ancestors of Han Jin arrested and executed. However, this did not help. The history books of future junctures changed to show that a new general rose to power, General He Jin, and did the same thing.

Events since then have suggested that we must capture sites with strong feng shui before any real changes of the time streams are possible. Unfortunately, interference from future warriors has hampered our efforts. Still, I have managed to push back General He Jin's attack until 189 A.D.

We have time to solidify our hold on this juncture, and time to conquer others. Because we reside in the earliest juncture presently open, we need not fear that other factions will conquer an earlier time and wipe us out. We shall build our power base, extend our tendrils down the halls of time, and I swear to you that I will live to see the Lotus become the masters of all human history.

A cold rain fell. Hoi Mao Qian crouched under the rim of a low ditch, his brother Vassals beside him. It had been two weeks since he slept in a real bed – since he had eaten real food.

This was, of course, the Old Man's fault. He said that Mao's abilities had progressed nicely. That he should harden them in battle. And now Mao stood ankle-deep in mud – cold, hungry and waiting to die.

The Fire Squad's leader, a swordsman named Chi Chui, whistled for the Vassals' attention. He did not say a word. He simply pointed toward the bandit camp, then nodded. A second later, he scrambled from his hiding place and raced across the short stretch of open ground. The others struggled to keep up, Mao lagging behind.

Cries of alarm rose from among the circular, felt tents. (Tents like those used by the Hsiung-nu, Mao thought.) But the bandits barely had time to grab their weapons before the Vassals hit. Chi Chui cut a swath through them, the other warriors poured in behind. Mao tried to keep himself near the back, safely away from the bandit's blades.

He wore a sword at his side, like all the Vassals, but he had not bothered to draw it. Nor did they expect him to.

Suddenly one of the bandits slashed his way through the Vassals' line. Waving his bloodied sword overhead, it charged Mao.

This was not like his classes. He did not have time to think, to prepare. He did not have time for control. Grabbing the magical energy at hand, Mao hurled it at his attacker. The bolt struck the bandit in the head. Within seconds, its energy had closed his mouth, nose and eyes – transmuting his face into a featureless flat surface. The bandit fell to the ground, writhing and clawing at his own skin.

Mao could still feel the power surging through his body. Nothing else seemed to matter. Not the cold, not the rain. Lashing out again and again, he let the power pour through him. His high-pitched laughter rang out above the camp.

Perhaps the Old Man was right after all.

CHAPTER 3

Current Activities

The Secret War

So they've finally sent you to me, eh? Well, you should feel honored. Few students reach this far. Few are privy to the secrets of the future and our battle throughout time. Well, find a seat. Make yourself comfortable. We have much to discuss.

Almost immediately after Meng Jen's discovery of the Netherworld, we learned that several factions fought for control over the time streams — indeed, over reality itself. Gao Zhang insisted that we learn more about these enemies before becoming tangled in their affairs. Unfortunately, our position in history has made this difficult. Others can look to history books for their clues about us and our juncture — we do not have that luxury.

Instead, Gao Zhang sent spies into the Netherworld and each Juncture. Though the information they returned seems to be a web of disinformation and half-truths, a hazy image has begun to appear.

The Architects of the Flesh

These sorcerers from the future became our first enemy. They came into our time to steal our demons, ghosts and spirits. However,

The Architects of the Flesh have the infamous honor of introducing the Lotus to the secret war. Much like Pandora, they released a hoard of demons upon the innocent. Fortunately, they have also become one of the Lotus's favorite targets.

With their technology, Arcanowave magic and abominations, the Architects seem to have the edge in these battles. However, Gao Zhang has a few advantages of his own. First, the Architects' hands are bound. They dare not casually interfere with the Lotus's natural growth and development, least they trigger a critical shift and erase themselves from history. Unlike our own time, the Architects to not want to capture the 69 juncture. They only use it as a mine for raw materials.

Second, many Lotus sorcerers have learned to summon and bind the Architects' abominations. In recent battles, many Buro field commanders watched their tactics crumble when a squad of their enhanced abominations turned and fired on their own troops. Often these super-soldiers recover shortly after the battle, as the years of brainwashing overcome the sorcerer's influence. However, many are captured by the Lotus and magically reprogrammed. These permanently join their ranks — at least until the Architects repeat the process.

An interesting dynamic has grown from this. Each side continues to capture and steal the other's prime warriors. I suppose this is the price they pay for relying on supernatural assistance. Still, the irony of the situation is not lost on either Gao Zhang or Johann Bonengel.

However, the deepest irony escapes them both. In many ways the Lotus and the Architects are similar. Both desire the spread of magic. They both sit atop an all-pervading, bureaucratic government. They both thrive in heavily-ordered and controlled societies.

If they ever decided to join forces, the resulting power would be nearly unstoppable. Thank God they hate each other so much.

— Dr. John Haynes, Dragon Observer, Full-Contact Historian and High-Caliber Anthropologist

The Old Man, eunuch scholar

Attributes: Bod 4, Chi 5 (Mag 8), Mnd 9, Ref 4
Skills: Info/Future History 17, Info/Imperial History 15, Info/Imperial Politics 15, Info/Lotus Politics 14, Info/Netherworld 14, Info/Secret War 16, Martial Arts 14, Sorcery 20
Sorcery Schticks: Divination, Signature Weapon (Staff)
Base Damage: 10 (staff)
Notes: After the discovery of the Netherworld, the Old Man maneuvered his way up the Metal division by pioneering the study of future history. He remains an influential power there. His minions travel throughout every juncture, feeding him threads of information. From these he weaves a tapestry of tangled interactions and power struggles. He builds a broad, all-encompassing picture.

after their incompetence allowed us to uncover the gateways through time, we began sending Fire Squads into their world.

In just two years, we have fought them here, in the Netherworld, and in every future we visit. These battles have become some of the most bloody and wasteful. But Gao has no intention of beating them through combat. No, they command a sprawling bureaucracy, much like our own Empire. As we seized control in this time, so shall we seize control over the future. We will find and exploit the corruption festering within their government. We will siphon off their power to feed ourselves.

As Gao so poetically said, we are gardeners. Today we plant the seeds of the Architects' destruction. Soon they will grow and bloom. Already the Movement of the Twined Snakes has allowed us to replace many of their operatives with our own shape-shifting demons.

Jade Wheel Society

By examining the histories of the future, we discovered several very interesting trends. One is the Jade Wheel Society and their Western counterpart, the Order of the Wheel.

As you know, we descended from the transformed animals in the 69 juncture. Back then, both sorcerers and priests considered transformed animals evil — abominations of nature. Our ancestors lived in constant fear. Should anyone discover their true nature, death followed swiftly.

To protect themselves, our ancestors banded together in secret. The first organizations were loose groups of a similar species, huddling together for safety. Then the renegade dragons showed the way. These individual circles combined with others, like links in a great chain. Soon, these chains matured into the Jade Wheel Society and the Order of the Wheel.

For the most part, the transformed animals of 69 A.D. care little about the secret war. They are only interested in securing a human life for themselves in their home juncture. Some, however, recognize a kinship with the lodge members from both the 1850 and contemporary junctures. Angered by their treatment at human hands, they gladly aid our pledged operatives.

The Lotus and their magic represents one of our greatest threats. We must do everything we can to ensure their eventual defeat. Ideally, I would like to destroy the Lotus and eliminate all Magic from the 69 juncture, but such action would damage the time lines — possibly erasing ourselves from history. Instead, we must try to contain the Lotus, keeping them from spreading to any other junctures.

Our operatives constantly scan both the 1850 and the contemporary junctures for Lotus activity. Any sign of infestation is quickly and ruthlessly stamped out.

— *Edward Knight, Bat Spy*

Both conspiracies begin in the twelfth century. Slowly, over centuries of patient expansion, they seized control of important trade routes and key persons — both in government and in business.

They are responsible for the eventual degradation of our great Empire. They allow China to grow stale, forcing it to turn in upon itself. They then bring Western merchants and their opium.

More than any others, these deserve our attention. We must learn more about them, their lodges and pledged warriors, if we hope to extend our current golden age throughout all time.

The Dragons

No matter where we go, here or in other junctures, there is always one constant: a ready stream of rabble-rousers eager to knock heads with our Vassals. At first, we gave them no notice. Gao has struggled against fed-up, righteous persons since his days as an imperial magistrate.

However, some of these seem different. They associate themselves with the heroic Silver Dragons of legend. No, I don't know why. After all, the Silver Dragons died — and died horribly. Still, some have taken the Dragons' name and continue to fight the Dragons' fight.

I hesitate to call them a faction. They aren't. Not like the Architects or Guiding Hand. Still, some individuals deserve special attention. Johnny Tso, Jack Donovan, Iala Mané, and Mad Dog McCroun, among others. They have a particularly irritating knack for thwarting our activities in the contemporary juncture. For that reason, we keep a careful eye on them and their associates.

Fortunately, many of these individuals died during the struggle over the Red Lantern Tavern. Unfortunately, Jueding Shelun and the Thing with 1,000 Tongues also perished. Not terribly surprising — Jueding always seemed a bit unstable.

The Four Monarchs

Both the Eaters of the Lotus and the Four Monarchs share a desire to spread magic across all junctures. But don't believe that we work together — or even trust one another. True, few conflicts have arisen. Despite their dream of returning, the Monarchs remain largely trapped within the Netherworld. We, on the other hand, use the Netherworld as little more than a highway to other junctures. Unless our presence there grows, we will continue to ignore one another.

Some Lotus members seem aware of our organization. Others do not, treating us as isolated individuals. This is good, it gives us an edge. We can organize attacks they will not possibly expect.

At this point, I don't believe any of the Lotus know about Kar Fai and the Prof. I hope to keep it that way.

— Dr. John Haynes, Dragon Observer, Full-Contact Historian and High-Caliber Anthropologist

Ming I: Queen of the Darkness Pagoda

Ming I is the only Monarch with whom we maintain regular contact. Early during our exploration, Gao Zhang arranged an alliance with her. If you find yourself in trouble while visiting the Netherworld, look to the Darkness Pagoda for help — but expect to pay a high price.

The relationship between Ming I and Gao Zhang is based on deceit and mutual betrayal. They share a grudging respect for each other, a respect largely tainted with envy. Though they have worked together for short-term gains, each inevitably tries to outmaneuver the other. Betrayal is commonplace — and easily forgiven.

— Moosh, Netherworld Scout

The King of the Fire Pagoda's natural understanding of human frailties has proven particularly useful against the Lotus. In their few struggles, Li Ting has always managed to exploit the inherent weaknesses in Lotus operatives. He continually seizes victory, even when strongly outnumbered. Fortunately for Gao, Li Ting has little interest in the Eaters of the Lotus.

— Moosh, Netherworld Scout

Though Pui Ti has yet to act against the Lotus, she keeps careful watch on their coming and going. She knows that Gao has a manipulative mind. Eventually, he will join the game of Inner Kingdom politics. Then she will act.

— Moosh, Netherworld Scout

Huan Ken, King of the Thunder Pagoda

The King of the Thunder Pagoda is a dimwitted, power-hungry twit. Gao Zhang despised him from the moment they met. When Huan Ken captured six of our sorcerers and burned them as heretics, the relationship took a further turn downwards.

However, Gao has carefully concealed his anger. Learn from this example. Battling Huan Ken would just waste lives. Instead, Gao hopes to trick him into fighting one of our battles for us — sacrificing his followers for our cause.

Li Ting, King of the Fire Pagoda

The King of the Fire Pagoda is a worthy opponent. He understands strength and the proper use of power. He commands a cadre of fierce warriors. Think carefully before earning their wrath. Fire may be a useful tool, but should it rage out of control, it will burn everything in its path.

Pui Ti, Queen of the Ice Pagoda

The Queen of the Ice Pagoda is weak — beneath our contempt. She huddles in her Pagoda, afraid of stepping outside.

The Guiding Hand

It is no secret that the Guiding Hand abhor us. Hiding behind their infinite, narrow-minded smugness, they accuse Gao Zhang of corruption and excess. They blame him for imperial china's growing weakness. If they would only open their eyes, they would see the lies behind their words. The fall came after us. We set the Empire on the path of greatness. We are the golden age!

Still, Quan Lo continues to send teachers and priests back to our juncture. These vile snakes turn the common folk against us. They encourage revolution against our rightful rule.

We must find these snakes before their deception spreads. The future of the Empire depends on it.

By sending teachers into the past, Quan Lo hopes to instill a sense of social order in both the Emperor and the populace. In this way, he plans to build a perfect empire that will last throughout all ages. Since the 69 juncture is culturally similar to Quan Lo's time, his operatives easily blend in. This, more than anything else, has Gao Zhang very nervous. Gao sees the Hand in every shadow.

As he should. The Hand have won the support of many members within the imperial bureaucracy. They have even arranged the appointment of Guiding Hand members into the Central Authority. Of course, the fierceness of the Hand's attacks only heighten Gao's fear. Unlike many other factions, they have no need to pull punches.

Fortunately for Gao, both the Ascended and the Architects want to keep his juncture intact. Each has operatives in the 69 Juncture, dedicated to rooting out and destroying all Hand influences.

Unfortunately, these operatives have difficulty distinguishing between Hand teachers and the political critics indigenous to Gao's time. Erring on the side of safety, they have eliminated many voices that might otherwise moderate Gao's rule.

— Dr. John Haynes, Dragon Observer, Full-Contact Historian and High-Caliber Anthropologist

Jammers

The Jammers must die. We should hack up their bodies to feed the dogs, then hang their heads from the tallest tree as a warning to other extremists. They are an abomination, hostile to our very way of life — perhaps to all life. I believe, if they succeed in destroying all magic and Chi, life itself will wither and die.

Sure, the Architects and Ascended might annoy, irritate and even frustrate Gao Zhang. The Hand has caused its share of paranoia and worry. I have even heard his minions curse some of our order. But so far, only the Jammers have managed to cause red-faced, vein-bulging, full-bore fury.

Given the Jammers' intent to wipe out all sources of magic and chi, the feng shui sites in ancient China have become prime targets. They have already struck a half-dozen important sites, and numerous smaller ones as well. Each time, Gao felt a bit of his influence slip away. Underlings began to grow more mischievous. Rumors and accusations, previously kept well away from the imperial palace, began to reach the Emperor's ear.

In one particularly vicious attack, the Jammers killed two sorcerers, sixteen swordsmen, a horned demon, an ogre and a host of walking dead. They then reduced the Temple of 10,000 Cats to a pile of ash. The next day — without even knowing of the Jammer attack — a faction of the Lotus broke away under the leadership of Hei Chih, a medium for the demon lord Sixteen-Fires. It was the loss of chi caused by the destruction of the temple that unknowingly spurred Hei Chih's group to rebel.

Gao spent two months fighting this rebellion, and another two patching the damage to his chi power structure.

The Jammer's attacks are also highly efficient. Like the Hand, they do not pull punches. They do not care about the time streams. In fact, they desire change. The Jammers don't worry about protecting or holding territory, save their bolt-holes in the Netherworld. They arrive, smack their target and leave. All objectives are limited and precise. After achieving their goal, they disappear back into the Inner Kingdom.

Gao Zhang has sworn vengeance against the Jammers. Those that he captures endure weeks of torture before having their disemboweled remains cast back into the Netherworld. Meanwhile, his forces are mustering for a massive retaliatory strike. Several others have agreed to join in the attack. Magic or Chi-using DPs flooded to his call. The Queen of the Darkness Pagoda promised the assistance of her Darkness Priestesses. I have even heard rumors of Architect involvement.

Gao hopes to cripple the Jammers with one blow. He plans to kill off their leaders and scatter the remaining force. He even bargained with the Lords of the Underworld, preparing a special Hell for Battlechimp Potemkin's soul.

However, others in the Inner Kingdom have also noticed the upcoming battle. Li Ting convinced his brother, Huan Ken, to assist the Jammers. Many suspect that the King of the Fire Pagoda will aid them as well. Meanwhile, Pui Ti watches the whole affair with growing amusement, and may well get involved.

If I were you, I'd stay away from the Netherworld for a while. At least until this blows through.

— Dr. John Haynes, Dragon Observer, Full-Contact Historian and High-Caliber Anthropologist

The Home Front

When Gao Zhang learned about the Lotus's collapse and the fall of his eunuch bureaucracy, he fell uncharacteristically quiet. For nearly a week, he roamed the palace, lurking in the background and brooding. Then further reports confirmed the initial information, and Gao burst into action. Private soldiers immediately marched from the palace grounds. Within an hour, they had gathered five of Han Jin's great grandfathers – all boys or young men.

Gao did not bother with a trial. The five arrived in chains. By nightfall their decapitated bodies lay outside Lo-yang's walls. Our future historians returned to their study, looking for descriptions of our continued greatness. But unfortunately, the assassinations only altered the details of our fall. History remained largely untouched.

This inability to alter time has continually plagued Gao. He knows that our position should give us great power. We only need to send a few spies forward. Armed with knowledge they bring back, we could act within our own juncture – where our forces are strongest – and bend the time streams according to our whims.

True changes only seem possible through the seizure of feng shui sites. Those of the Metal division have conducted elaborate experiments on the time streams and the Netherworld. We have even pushed back

As you can see, the Lotus have made more enemies than friends. This is partially the nature of the Secret War. Factions do not trust one another, and alliances are short-term agreements with specific objectives.

Even so, Gao Zhang and his followers are particularly-difficult to work with. The Eaters of the Lotus tend to be deranged megalomaniacs. They see themselves as inherently superior to any others. Though more broad-minded than the Hand, China remains the heart of their world and from what they have seen, the 69 juncture is the height of Chinese civilization. They believe that their "superior nature" gives them the unquestionable right to rule all time. While they can find their share of like-minded underlings and toadying lackeys, few Secret Warriors willingly endure their condescending attitude.

— Dr. John Haynes, Dragon Observer, Full-Contact Historian and High-Caliber Anthropologist

our (for now) eventual destruction by six decades! But the ability to erase our enemies still eludes us.

Some claim this is due to interference from other factions. True, the Order of the Wheel and the Jade Wheel Society move to defend important sites, while the Hand and Jammers attack those we already own. And the damned Dragons always appear at the most inconvenient moments. But this is not the whole truth.

They can only slow us down. Each faction has its own plots, schemes and struggles to worry about. Besides, the 69 juncture is our stronghold.

The truth is, our stronghold remains somewhat unstable. Be careful who you repeat that to, child. Gao would take off your head for just thinking it. However, the facts remain. We do not yet have an iron grip over our juncture. There are many enemies and obstacles lurking within the home front.

Bureaucracy

Many members of the Empire's bureaucracy naturally resent our influence, though their instinct for self-preservation usually exceeds any feelings of righteous outrage.

Most bureaucrats, in fact most Chinese, accept a certain amount of corruption. No one likes it, but they see it as inevitable. Getting things done always involves bribery or an exchange of favors.

So they do not necessarily mind our manipulations — simply the extent to which we take them. Or, more typically, the fact that we are receiving bribes that would otherwise line their coffers. Oh, you will find a few idealists who believe they can right all wrongs, but these inevitably turn up missing or dead. Most officers take a more pragmatic view.

Don't fool yourself. If we give them an opportunity, they will act to increase their power or reduce our own. However, as long as they are kept on a tight leash, they will spend most of their time ignoring the problems. They do not want to risk their own position or power.

Remember: Those who have climbed the ladder of state have always accepted bribes — at least at some level. From his earliest days in the palace, Gao had a handful of officials in his pay. Now that he has the power to secure bureaucratic appointments and raise people up the ranks, his official support has grown. Many willingly accept his rule, in exchange for these rewards.

Few, however, offer their support openly. Too many scholars and everyday citizens com-

Though few officials actually threaten Gao's power, their continual infighting is a steady drain on his resources. The Lotus constantly watch for the growth of unsavory alliances. They need to protect themselves against betrayal, and they need to keep their officials happy. Often a number of "loyal" officials will desire the same position. The resulting appointments require great diplomacy and negotiation.

— Dr. John Haynes, Dragon Observer, Full-Contact Historian and High-Caliber Anthropologist

plain about our excesses. They blame us for their own shortcomings. The officials, therefore, publicly decry Gao's actions, while secretly obeying his orders. This has an interesting side effect. An outraged peasant never knows where to turn for help. Their complaints may find a truly helpful ear — but, more often, the information is passed on to us. We can then remove the traitor at our leisure.

Empress Jui Szu

Empress Jui Szu is a continual stone in our shoe. Don't overestimate her. She has no real power — Gao made sure of that. But she remains visible and active within Lo-yang. Many disagree with the charges against her. Especially now, as Harvest of Jade grows old, they feel her son was his rightful heir — cut down by palace politics. (If only they knew the truth, eh?)

Some use her name as a banner. They rally around the idea of her. Many of these are zealots, willing to throw away their lives in glorious, meaningless acts of terrorism.

Bandits

Imperial Doctrine states that Bandits are a serious threat to the future of the Empire. They plague the roads throughout China. Instead of pursuing an honorable career like farming, or even a somewhat suspicious occupation like jade carving or merchanting, they choose to live off of what they can steal from isolated villages and travelers.

Realize, of course, this is only partially the truth. Bandits do cause problems for officials and citizens alike; however, many of them are in our employ — or somebody else's. Most Bandits eagerly accept the protection of a strong patron. This gives them a source of supplies, a base of operations and a place to hide.

Still, bandits are, by nature, individualistic. Most no longer believe in the Confucius hierarchy or the rules of Legalism. They only listen to the rules of strength and profit.

Though most officials present little opposition to the Lotus, Empress Jui Szu and her faction still exert a great influence on China's politics. This is not too surprising. Though she has left the imperial palace, the Empress still oversees many official functions. On the practical side, this means that she has remained attuned to many of the Empire's powerful feng shui sites.

Empress Jui Szu has created her own web-work power structure within the Central Authority. The initial structure came from the discontented flocking to her side. The Order of the Empress — the remnant of Empress Lu's rebellion — met with her the day she left the imperial palace. However, Jui Szu has built upon this foundation. Her friends and personal contacts reach through all levels of the imperial bureaucracy. She has further forged alliances with many officials in exile — particularly those recently removed by Gao Zhang.

Like Gao's supporters, few officials openly declare their allegiance to the Empress. However, unlike Gao's, these officials obey her out of loyalty and faith. They are drawn by the strength of her personality — not bribes and the promise of power.

Unfortunately, the Empress cannot yet move openly. She has seen too many allies destroyed, either by Gao's hired thugs, by imperial decree or by supernatural horrors. Instead, she bides her time. She continues to extend her web. She stabs now and then, when she sees a weakness, but is otherwise content to wait and prepare.

Though hesitant to move against Gao, the Empress actively protects people from his wrath. She helps relocate fugitives to distant provinces, where Gao's power remains weak. She arranges aid for cities besieged by Gao's emergency taxation or by supernatural attack.

Empress Jui Szu knows about Gao's power over the other eunuchs and his strength within the bureaucracy. She also knows about his supernatural support. However, she remains ignorant about the Eaters of the Lotus, the Netherworld and the Secret War. Her enemy is Gao and his supporters, not a secret society. She wants to place one of her family on the Dragon Throne, but has no desire to conquer all of time.

— *Tu Shih, Hand Infiltrator and Scholar*

Don't turn your back on them, especially if you have cash in your purse.

Few people choose to become bandits. Most are unfortunates, driven from their land by natural disaster, over-taxation or imperial decree. Lacking any legitimate means to make a living, they resort to banditry.

Some prosper in this new lifestyle, growing rich and powerful. They soon earn a name throughout the region, and a following of other dispossessed souls. Others fail. Their mutilated bodies hang beside the imperial highways as a warning to others.

Many bandits will aid any attempt to harm the Empire or Gao Zhang. However, they have long lived outside the bounds of law and society. They will not bow to any leader, save those that rise from their own ranks. They are also untrusting, and should not be trusted.

— Dr. John Haynes, Dragon Observer, Full-Contact Historian and High-Caliber Anthropologist

Arygh, Hsiung-nu chief

Attributes: Bod 8, Chi 0, Mnd 5, Ref 6
Skills: Drive (horse) 15, Guns 17, Info/Tactics 17, Martial Arts 16
Schticks: Eagle Eye, Fast Draw x2, Lightning Reload, Signature Weapon (bow)
Base Damage: 12 (sword), 10 (bow)
Notes: Arygh has just seized control over the Keretis tribe. He promises to return the Hsiung-nu to their former glory and has already led a half-dozen raids into China. Meanwhile, other blood-hungry youth rush to his side — his numbers have doubled in the last six months. If this continues, the Keretis will outshine all other tribes on the steppes. When Arygh rides, he typically has ten mounted warriors at his side — more when raiding.

Hsiung-nu unnamed warrior

Attributes: Bod 6, Chi 0, Mnd 4, Ref 6
Skills: Drive (horse) 12, Guns 11, Martial Arts 8
Base Damage: 10 (sword), 7 (bow)

Hsiung-nu

The Hsiung-nu are nomadic tribes of barbarians, living in the windswept plains off the Empire's northwest frontier. Nearly born in the saddle, they spend more time on a horse than off. Their riding skill remains unsurpassed, and their fighting prowess follows close behind. They are the Empire's greatest indigenous threat.

Gao Zhang knows that eventually a prince will rise among them. After gaining nomination as chief of the Mangkhol tribe, Chengiz Khan will cut a bloody path through the steppes. Whereas now, inter-tribal war keeps the Hsiung-nu weak, Chengiz will unite them under one banner. His motto, "One sun in the sky, one sovereign on earth," sets the tone for his rule. With two quick offensives, he conquers all of China, then turns his sight westward. By the time of his death, the entire world lies at his feet.

Though future Chinese will eventually assimilate their barbarian overlords, the continuing cycle of foreign occupation will leave them weak and unable to withstand Western domination.

But now, the Hsiung-nu wear animal skins and drink the blood of their enemy from human skulls. They have tasted the wealth of the Empire. Seeking silks, jade and grain, they sweep out of the northern plains to raid small towns and military outposts along the frontier.

Sorcerers

We are not the only sorcerous secret society. Mystery cults flourish throughout the Empire, the White Lotus being the most famous. They, and other societies like them, remain curiously uninterested in worldly

The Empire has long fought the Hsiung-nu. They fortified their northwest frontier with troops and built the Great Wall (though in their arrogance, the Hsiung-nu claim that the wall holds China in, protecting the steppes). They have even tried to buy peace — with limited success.

While the Hsiung-nu may admire the goods that flow from the Empire, they have little respect for the Chinese people. They find them weak and cannot understand why they willingly live as prisoners, trapped within their cities and towns.

The Hsiung-nu currently abide by a treaty signed when Harvest of Jade was still a powerful battlefield commander. Now that the Emperor has grown frail and passive, a lust for battle has re-emerged among the clans. Many argue that the agreement no longer binds. The Emperor is a spineless coward and no longer deserves their respect.

While the clan elders have kept the peace, the hot-blooded youth are gaining support. Already, two clans have broken with their leader's wishes, launching raids against the southlands.

— Dr. John Haynes, Dragon Observer, Full-Contact Historian and High-Caliber Anthropologist

power — seeking only personal enlightenment and spiritual purity. Future history tells us that, due to imperial persecution, the White Lotus will eventually sink from their lofty ideals, finding refuge in organized crime. After a brief stay with the Shaolin (and the Guiding Hand), they will escape to found the Triads. Over time, the last traces of mysticism dissolve, only commemorated by hazy initiation rites.

Taoists

Though I could say many things about the Taoists, they are probably best characterized by the paradoxes that surround them. They recommend accepting life as it is, living each moment in tune with nature. However, they also pursue the perfection of the spirit, supernatural powers and even immortality. They frequently assume the role of pacifists, not even defending themselves against attacks — but

Most of the ancient mystery cults are uninterested in the Eaters of the Lotus. When questioned about the eunuch sorcerers, they smile and say that fraternization with demons brings its own punishment. They will not fight for our cause.

But that does not mean we cannot use them. While these sorcerers maintain their detachment towards Lotus abuses in Lo-yang or in distant provinces, detachment frequently turns to outrage when the eunuchs interfere with their communities.

— Tu Shih, Hand Infiltrator and Scholar

These mischievous, whimsical sages and teachers live throughout all of China. As the leaders of the second major belief system, they offer a mystical viewpoint to augment Confucian logic and hierarchy.

— Dr. John Haynes, Dragon Observer, Full-Contact Historian and High-Caliber Anthropologist

Sometimes the Taoists begin organizing rebellions against the Empire itself. This is usually the result of heaven withdrawing its mandate from a corrupt Emperor. Heaven indicates this loss through famine, epidemic, earthquake, drought or flood. Unfortunately, due to China's temperamental environment, such natural disasters are common. As soon as Gao defeats a rebellion in one province, another starts. A particularly troublesome trend, since Gao's typical method of quelling resistance — demonic infestation — only further supports the Taoist claims.

So far, Taoist involvement in either form, has done lit tle real harm to Gao's power. Individual interference rarely lasts longer than a few months. It is annoying, like the bite of a mosquito or sting of a wasp, but it has little effect in the long term.

Taoist-inspired rebellions are a slightly different story. Except in the most extreme situations, the Taoists gather few people to their side, and the imperial army quickly puts down any resistance they might offer. Still, the rebellions force Gao to ship resources and aid to the Empire's troubled areas, lest the people rebel in serious numbers. Of course, this may have been the Taoists' goal all along.

— Tu Shih, Hand Infiltrator and Scholar

I remember a team of hired thugs that patrolled the Kwangtung province, extracting Gao's emergency taxation from the populace. Ten Badger Hill, a wandering Taoist priest, arrived in the village of Lu-chih, just after the raiding party passed through. Learning of the villagers' plight, Ten Badger Hill decided to teach the thugs a lesson.

Seeking out Wang Hu, the bandit's leader, Ten Badger asked to join their band. Being a large man, built like a bear, he easily impressed Wang with various feats of strength. He smashed stones with his hands and defeated their strongest warrior in a wrestling match.

Wang Hu greedily accepted Ten Badger Hill's aid. He believed their raids would grow more successful with this new might at his command. Of course, Ten Badger's "assistance" came at an unusual price.

At each meal, Ten Badger ate enough for six people, quickly draining the band's supplies. Acting the idiot, he botched any task they assigned to him — usually creating a tangle that took Wang days to fix. For example, on his first raid, Wang told Ten Badger to fill the wagons with as much rice as he could. Ten Badger obeyed, filling the wagons, until their axles broke under the weight. When Wang discovered the problem, the bandit leader screamed at Ten Badger. "What have you done? What do you think you're doing?"

Ten Badger simply smiled back and said, "I'm loading the wagons, like you asked. I could probably put more rice on them, but I'm worried that they might get stuck in the mud."

Ten Badger Hill also repeated off-hand comments, making sure that harsh words reached the wrong ears. For example, he proudly told Wang that his first lieutenant, Keui, obviously held a great respect for their leader. "He said you were like no other man under heaven. That you had as much wisdom as the rock underfoot — an honor, I'm sure, since the rocks have witnessed every event since the dawn of time...no, I'm positive he meant to honor you with those words. He was very specific, you see: after comparing you to a rock, he said that it was a compliment."

Within a month, Ten Badger Hill had bogged down the bandits, preventing them from accomplishing anything. Soon, angry messages began arriving from the imperial palace. Gao wanted his taxes and would not listen to any excuse.

Wang realized that he needed to get rid of Ten Badger. He ordered Ten Badger to leave the group, but Ten Badger refused to abandon his "leader and friend." He tried to move their camp while Ten Badger was away on a mission, hoping to leave the brute behind. But Ten Badger followed along like a lost puppy. He even ordered his men to attack Ten Badger, but the monk grew overjoyed at the "training" and proceeded to pound the bandits senseless.

Eventually, Gao reached the end of his patience. Imperial guards arrived in the Kwangtung province, arresting and executing Wang and the bandits. However, when the troops arrived, Ten Badger Hill was suspiciously absent.

— Dr. John Haynes, Dragon Observer, Full-Contact Historian and High-Caliber Anthropologist

their voices quickly rise against imperial oppression of the common folk.

Though some live within cities and farming communities, others seek solitary lives in nature. As far as I am concerned, these are the most dangerous. Through meditation and spiritual refinement, they gain great chi or magical abilities.

Fortunately, these hermits rarely involve themselves in our affairs. They simply wish to remain isolated and at peace. Still, they openly disapprove of the imperial hierarchy and laws.

Ten Badger Hill, taoist monk

Attributes: Bod 9, Chi 7, Mnd 5, Ref 6

Skills: Info/Animals 8, Info/Food 12, Info/Survival 10, Martial Arts 16

Schticks: Clothed in Life, Armored in Life, Crane Stance, Wing of the Crane, Beak of the Crane, Talon of the Crane.

Base Damage: 10 (punch) 11 (kick)

They see its Confucian politeness and obligations as an abomination of nature.

Also, They frequently come to the aid of local people, though they always limit this to a specific problem, and it rarely comes in an expected form.

Supernatural Creatures

A wide variety of supernatural creatures wander our countryside. Many, like the hungry ghosts, ogres and demons, willingly serve our cause. Others oppose us or are, at best, neutral.

Of course, the more powerful the supernatural creature, the less likely they are to notice human affairs. The Jade Emperor may rule over a vast hierarchy of gods, but he cares little for the day-to-day actions of human beings. He delegated those responsibilities to subordinates, who likewise delegated them to subordinates.

Consequently, local spirits and gods have the most contact with humans. These may be minor powers, but they frequently have a vested interest in local affairs. As long as a village or household maintains the proper rituals, these spirits and gods protect them. Therefore, our sorcerers must often corrupt an area, driving off these beneficial powers, before we can send in our supernatural forces.

However, a discussion of the full breadth of supernatural influences must wait for another day.

Securing

You can divide our goals into two main classifications: securing our current holdings, and expanding our influence.

To secure our power, Gao uses a combination of informants, bribes and brutal attacks. He trusts no one — not even his allies and underlings.

For this reason, feng shui professors, fortune tellers and spirit mediums track various trends in the Lotus's fortune. Unfortunately, these methods have met with limited success. They can spot general threats and potential problems, but fail to pick out specifics. A clear image often comes only after the enemy begins to act.

Mortal spies and informants are a little more reliable — but they can only watch suspected threats. Consequently, Gao uses them to follow up on his supernatural leads. By combining both methods, Gao and the Petals receive a generally-useful understanding of important trouble spots.

When facing immediate danger, the Petals often try to buy off the threat. Gao knows that combat is risky and unpredictable. Anytime he sends the Lotus into battle, there's a chance we will not come back. Still, he recognizes that bribes are only a temporary patch. You cannot trust purchased loyalty. The bribes should

> Like many of Gao's instructions, his guidelines on bribes are a sound idea, but utterly unworkable in the real world. Trying to respond to every threat would spread the Lotus dangerously thin. Therefore, they often let minor problems slide — sometimes for years — while they concentrate their forces elsewhere. Meanwhile, they rely on these "stop-gap" bribes to keep the peace.
>
> In some cases, these bribes have become institutionalized. They are a fact of life — like taxes.
>
> *— Tu Shih, Hand Infiltrator and Scholar*
>
> The Eaters of the Lotus pay lip service to economy when dealing with threats. Gao insists that they use the minimum expenditure of force and resources necessary; however, given the volatile nature of his underlings, these responses often escalate to ridiculous levels. While the Pillars of Heaven spot and identify the worst cases, many irate underlings vent their anger upon innocents.
>
> *— Dr. John Haynes, Dragon Observer, Full-Contact Historian and High-Caliber Anthropologist*

Despite the variety of forces opposing Lotus control, few offer any real challenge to their rule. Yes, this opposition often chews up valuable resources and time, but the Lotus continue to grow and expand.

Ironically, Gao suspects that the greatest threat to his organization may come from within. He knows that the loyalty of his underlings comes from greed and fear. They remain inherently untrustworthy, and he suspects — no, he expects them to plot against him. It is inevitable. Either their greed will outstrip the meager rewards he gives them, or their fear will disappear. Regardless, someone will try to grab the reigns for himself.

Of course, he also faces threats more subtle than outright rebellion. Like Gao himself, most Lotus members tend toward megalomania. They find it hard to control their desires. When given a little power, you can virtually guarantee that they'll abuse it.

Gao Zhang has learned through experience the dangers of uncontrolled greed. He has seen the destructive consequences both in his own life and in the history of the Ten Thousand Eyes. Though he finds self-control painfully difficult, he frequently pays it passing lip service. Of course, Gao's self-control usually starts with a wave of highly-touted, minor reforms and ends with excesses even more extreme than before.

Unfortunately, many of Gao's underlings lack even this twisted self-control. The only thing that stays their hand is the fear of their superiors. This frequently means that they overtax their regions and try to hide the excess money, keeping it for themselves. When the region inevitably protests, they try to handle the situation locally — refusing to alert their superiors. Because of this, much of the Empire teeters on the brink of open rebellion.

To counter these threats, Gao has created two similar, yet separate, branches. The first branch, the Silent Eyes, spy on their fellow Lotuses, searching out and exposing any treachery or disobedience. They answer to no one but Gao himself, and have the authority to capture, question, torture and execute whomever they please.

The second group, Pillars of Heaven, travel across the Empire, ensuring that local magistrates and Lotus squads do not abuse their power. They have unlimited authority to review the local taxation records and interview the populace.

Though actually a branch of the Lotus, the Pillars of Heaven ostensibly fall under the Emperor's direct control. They are a tool for uncovering corruption within his bureaucracy. In fact, the leader of the Pillars, Wan Qian, is not bound by imperial law or decree while performing his duties. He is the only person in the Empire that need not bow before the Emperor.

The knowledge that his head will never decorate Lo-yang's gates gives Wan the confidence to question any imperial decree — even those that originate from Gao Zhang. Still, he can not stretch this freedom too far. Wan knows full well the other methods at Gao's disposal. Besides, the Pillars of Heaven can only record and report. They cannot take action. Even were they to discover information damaging to Gao Zhang, Gao's control of the Emperor would probably protect him.

In order to insure the highest level of security, Gao has instructed both the Silent Eyes and the Pillars of Heaven to investigate each other. With everyone watching and being watched, no one dares step out of line.

Still, Gao spends an incredible amount of time consulting with demons, mediums and fortune tellers. He constantly watches over his shoulder, imagining new plots or conspiracies. He spends most of his money and power ensuring, if not the loyalty, then at least the behavior of those under his control.

— Dr. John Haynes, Dragon Observer, Full-Contact Historian and High-Caliber Anthropologist

act as a stopgap measure, buying enough time to muster our forces.

More important problems gain a more direct response. A single imperial edict often handles the small stuff. Strike teams, troubleshooting squads, divisions of the imperial army and summoned forces of darkness deal with the rest. Individual troublemakers find themselves arrested, discredited, erased or replaced by supernatural doubles. Monsters and natural disasters quickly besiege troublesome regions.

Of course, we have learned that all these plans and precautions mean little against the power of feng shui. I have seen how our destiny fluctuates based on the number of sites we control. When we gain more, rebellions dissolve and underlings show uncharacteristic restraint and loyalty. If someone should capture or destroy a site, the resulting shock wave can leave behind a tangle of disasters, deception and open conflict.

Though common wisdom tells leaders to consolidate their power, we must seize more

> There are five kinds of fire attack: burning people, burning supplies, burning equipment, burning storehouses, and burning weapons.
>
> The use of fire must have a basis, and requires certain tools. There are appropriate times for setting fires, namely when the weather is dry and windy.
>
> Generally, in fire attacks it is imperative to follow up on the crises caused by the fires. When the fire is set inside an enemy camp, then respond quickly from outside. If the soldiers are calm when the fire breaks out, wait — do not attack. When the fire reaches the height of its power, follow up if possible, hold back if not.
>
> — *Sun Tzu,* The Art of War, *translated by Thomas Clearly*

feng shui sites if we expect the Eaters of the Lotus to survive. This has led to aggressive expansion both here and in the other junctures.

Expansion

Gao and the Petals have developed strict guidelines for our expansion. However, like many guidelines, these represent an ideal. Restrictions on time and resources often demand adjustments to the grand plan. Furthermore, you cannot discount the personalities involved. Some leaders have a style that reaches beyond any guidance from above.

Expansion plans may originate from any command center, though most come from the Petals themselves. Few centers have the resources necessary to launch an attack on their own. Besides, Gao reacts harshly towards those defeated while pursuing unapproved goals. Only those with absolute confidence or unquenchable ambition will dare consider such action. The generals of other junctures are the only significant exception. Their separation demands a higher level of independence and initiative.

Regardless of their origins, all expansion plans begin with extensive intelligence operations. Gao Zhang has shown that knowledge is power. His control over information has stripped Harvest of Jade of all real authority. Gao, therefore, demands extensive knowledge about any situation before committing Lotus resources.

And the Wood division is all-too-eager to obey. They frequently stress the value of their operations. Not surprising since an expanded importance equals greater access to Lotus resources. Furthermore, eager Wood leaders hope to impress the Petals and gain promotions into the Water division.

As a result, the Wood division has grown into one of the Lotus's most successful branches. Their operatives have infiltrated every Juncture, and many powerful organizations. In the 69 juncture, they have spies planted in the Hsiung-nu, in Empress Jui Szu's court, and within the families whose descendants will eventually destroy the eunuch control.

However, spies are not enough. The planners must also consult various fortune tellers, mediums and feng shui professors from the Metal division. These mystics predict the venture's outcome, and point out key elements that might change the fortune. They also chart the best day and hour for the attack, ensuring the best chance for victory. Finally, the Metal division oversees a series of offerings and rituals aimed at gaining spiritual support.

Once the plans are finalized and rituals performed, one or more Fire squads go in. More like terrorists than a true army, these small groups of elite warriors strike the weak points in our enemy's defenses. They try to cripple the enemy, capturing the target if possible. At a minimum, they provide a beachhead for larger forces.

After the Fire squads open the door, forces from the Earth division arrive. These forces defeat any lingering resistance, then fortify our defenses. For the most part, they hold the ground that the Fire division hands them.

If the gains are important, the Water division then arrives, creating an on-site command center. Usually the first step in a series of conquests, these command centers act as a rally point for further operations. The Petals believe that our expansion should proceed through a series of limited steps. They imagine strings of command centers stretching out across china (and throughout time) like pearls on a necklace. Pointing out that the expansion more closely resembles a net or web only makes them mad. The Petals often hold more respect for poetry than accurate descriptions.

Other Junctures

In order to ease our expansion into other junctures, the Petals have established a general in each time. In theory, these generals act as an extension of the Petals, overseeing their will in each Juncture. In practice, they remain largely autonomous.

Despite impressive gains during the last two years, we remain relatively weak outside our own juncture. The Petals, therefore, hesitate before committing any new forces there. When they do send assistance, its typically earmarked for a specific mission planned and organized by the Petals themselves.

The generals, therefore, must manage our holdings using whatever means they can scrape together. On the positive side, they quickly become excellent recruiters, gathering new members from within the local community. On the negative side, they are always outnumbered and outgunned. For this reason, the generals keep a low profile. If our enemies discovered them, they would quickly die. Sure, the Inner Council could try to provide reinforcements, hoping to defend their holdings — but these would undoubtedly arrive too late.

Ironically, many of the other factions know specific members of the Fire division, since they constantly spar with these forces. They, of course, know about Gao Zhang and the other high-ranking members in the 69 juncture, but the puppet masters of the later junctures remain undiscovered.

1850

Water Thorn Cha Tzu is the general of the 1850 juncture. A quiet man, he enjoys sipping tea and studying classical texts. He lives in a modest estate just outside the International District of Shanghai with his wife and five children. His trade company operates throughout China. However, behind the unobtrusive mask of refined manners lurks a student of the black arts and an accomplished demonologist.

The Petals chose Cha Tzu because of his subtlety. He quietly pursues our interests, never drawing attention to himself or the Lotus. So far, he has established a number of safe houses for our operatives in China and Japan. His merchant caravans and trade ships allow him to move people and supplies about the country without drawing attention. He has even recruited several dozen new members from within the 1850 juncture — though they remain loyal to Cha Tzu, not Gao and the Petals.

Cha Tzu is also an accomplished businessman. His trading company works as a liaison between the foreign powers and the Chinese nationalists. He manages to support both sides, without offending either. One branch of his company exports tea, bringing Western currency and goods into China. Meanwhile, another secretly sells opium, further sapping the Empire's strength — preparing this juncture for our eventual takeover. Cha uses this trade as a weapon, specifically targeting families and regions that pose a threat to future activities. Opium is corruption given physical form — and, like all the Lotus, Cha understands the power of corruption.

Ironically, his business acumen has drawn the attention of both the Guiding Hand and the Order of the Wheel. Low ranking members of both organizations have approached Cha, hoping to win his support. The Guiding Hand wants his help to strengthen China against foreign intruders. They appeal to him as an upstanding citizen and a loyal servant of the Empire, not knowing of his opium trade.

Meanwhile, the Order of the Wheel see Cha Tzu as an aggressive and accomplished businessman. They appeal to his greed, offering him great wealth and business opportunities, in return for helping them spread their power and influence throughout the mainland.

Cha Tzu, water thorn of 1850

Attributes: Bod 4, Chi 2 (Mag 8), Mnd 8, Ref 5
Skills: Deceit 14, Detective 8, Info/Business Administration 12, Sorcery 18
Schticks: Blast (conjured weapons, disease, fire, object overload), Influence, Summoning
Base Damage: 10 (blast)

Cha Tzu currently remains open yet noncommittal to both offers. He hopes that both organizations will accept one of his underlings into their ranks, allowing Cha to infiltrate the enemy.

Cha Tzu's ambitions also spread beyond China's borders. He has used his business contacts to send many Lotus immigrants to the American west. While the west of gunslingers and desperadoes is still about fifteen years off (when the flood of civil war veterans enter the area) it is still a wild, lawless place. Future history has shown that Chinese immigrants will play a vital, though unappreciated, role in the region. By sending our operatives and their families during the early waves of immigration, Cha hopes to create a power base there.

Lotus members in the American west hope to seize some of the power that would otherwise go to Order of the Wheel tycoons, while improving the lot of Chinese immigrant workers. Don't let that fool you — Cha is not as altruistic as he sounds. After all, Cha Tzu willingly forces opium on his own people. Simply put, he believes his assistance will create a strong body loyal to our cause.

However, creating a power base has proven more difficult than anyone expected. Our operatives have already fought several conflicts with the indigenous tribes over the ownership of feng shui sites. These warriors have proven unexpectedly fierce, and their medicine men equal Cha's sorcerers.

This surprised Cha Tzu. He knows that the United States will roll over the native tribes with little effort, and so believed they were weak and helpless against assault. However, his defeats have proven differently. The United States Government will achieve its Manifest Destiny, not through superior fighting skill, but through the unstoppable force of their feng shui. Cha has identified several important sites already under their control.

Unfortunately, this means our forces will likewise be trampled under the weight of feng shui, unless he can create an alliance with the natives. With the bad blood already between us, any such alliance remains unlikely.

Penny Bane, contemporary Lotus mastermind

Attributes: Body 5, Chi 0 (For 6, Mag 10), Mnd 9, Ref 5
Skills: Deceit 15, Sorcery 14
Sorcery Schticks: Influence, Summoning
Base Damage: 12 (blast), 6 (fist)

Contemporary

Choosing a Lotus general for the contemporary juncture proved a difficult task. The first problem was the cultural differences. Lotus operatives often found the modern world confusing and awkward. Not understanding even basic technology, they quickly fell victim to security cameras and walkie-talkies. The limits on magic and supernatural creatures removed a great amount of our power. And no matter how hard we try,

eunuch sorcerers from 69 AD just do not blend into downtown Hong Kong.

Sure, the Petals sent small teams to handle specific jobs. We were fortunate enough to find and awaken the demonic island Kun Chau. But no one could establish a permanent base. That is, until we found Penny Bane. Penny is an American computer engineer working in Hong Kong. Her father practiced Chinese medicine in San Francisco. Her mother, an ex-hippy, attended Berkeley during the 60s. Penny (whose real name is Pen Hei) grew up surrounded by a potpourri of mysticism and rampant open-mindedness.

It is no wonder that Penny found herself drawn to the occult at a young age. She studied everything: witchcraft, Fu Kay, numerology, Tarot and acupuncture. She apprenticed herself to spirit mediums and new age crackpots. It was all harmless. No real power involved. No real harm done.

However, one day her spells started to work. She visited Tom Annis, a friend who was sick with pneumonia. Writing out a cure spell on yellow paper, Penny asked Tom to burn the spell and drink the ashes with a glass of water. Tom humored her, as he had many times before. But this time, to everyone's surprise, Tom began feeling better within minutes of activating the spell. The next day he returned to work, feeling refreshed and rested.

Two days later things began to get strange. Penny caught glimpses of men wearing gray pinstripe suits and dark sunglasses. They always seemed innocent, thumbing through the newspapers at a corner kiosk or buying hot dogs and pretzels from a vendor. But at least one always lurked in the background.

That night, when Penny returned to her apartment, she found the door knocked off its hinges and the inside trashed. Someone had pushed over her bookshelves, emptied her desk drawer and booted up her computer. The

Bob, weird hippy freak

Attributes: Bod 5, Chi 0 (For 8), Mnd 8, Ref 5
Skills: Detective 13, Infiltration 10, Info/Conspiracy Theories 15, Info/Secret War 12
Unique Schticks
Go to Ground: When Bob does not want to be found, no one finds him. No one. Anyone he hides is likewise safe — providing they follow his instructions.
Know Someone: No matter where he is, no matter what the problem, Bob knows someone who can help. Of course, there's no guarantee on the quality of this help.
Notes: Bob cannot take any action that directly harms a living creature. Yes, he is vegan. However, he will make an exception for walking corpses and other mindless dead things.

Popcorn Demons, unnamed fiends

Attributes: Bod 6, Chi 1, Mnd 4, Ref 5
Skills: Intimidation 8, Martial Arts 10
Creature Schtick: Blaze of Glory
Unique Schtick
Hard to Kill: When you knock out a Popcorn Demon, record th blow's outcome. After that many Sequences pass, the Popcorn Demon wakes up. You must kill them to take them out of the fight.
Base Damage: 7 (claws)
Notes: When Penny Bane discovered these demons, she quickly adopted them as her shock troops. She usually sends in twelve or so — just to soften the resistance. Though the Popcorn Demons have relatively weak fighting abilities, their tendency to explode when injured makes them deadly at close range. Note that any Popcorn Demon caught in another's Blaze of Glory will also die. When fighting in groups, they tend to go up in large chain reactions.

contents of her kitchen cabinets lay open and scattered across the floor. The itchy scent of flowers and mixed spices hung in the air like allergenic air-freshener.

The remains of her bed rested upturned on a pile of clothing torn from her closet and bureau. As if to add insult to injury, the intruders had stolen her diary and reformatted her computer's hard drive – erasing everything on it.

Fearing that she had unknowingly stepped on the mafia or triad's toes, Penny grabbed her toothbrush and a few changes of clothing, then set out to find a safe place to hide. And when it came to hiding, she could not think of anyone she trusted more than Bob, an old friend of her mother.

Bob typically dressed in faded bell-bottoms held together by a dozen patches, earth-tone tunics and Jesus sandals. He always carried a knit satchel which usually contained three different controlled substances. Most importantly, however, he was paranoid. Bob believed that everyone was out to get him – from NSA spooks to little green men from Alpha Centauri. When it came to hiding and avoiding unwanted attention, he knew it all.

After helping Penny move from San Francisco to an abandoned apartment in Seattle, Bob went out to study her mysterious pursuers. One week later he returned, claiming they were part of the Secret Spokemen. This conspiracy controlled everything, even the NSA spooks and little green men. And, if you believed the rumors, their direct supervisor was a mutant spider.

After a week of hiding in a cold dark basement and eating beanie-weenies straight from the can, Penny had already begun to feel a bit ridiculous. Then Bob began describing how the Spokemen killed Elvis after the King uncovered their secret plans. Something inside her snapped. The trouble in San Francisco was undoubtedly local. And even if not, she was safe in a new city. They would not find her here. Interrupting Bob in mid-rant, she left the apartment, determined to start a new life.

Much to Penny's surprise, four pledged members from the Order of the Wheel captured her less than two blocks from her hideout.

They bound her hands behind her back and tossed her into the back seat of a nondescript black van. The pledged jumped in, and they drove for hours. No one said a word.

Judging by the van's sound, they were cruising down the highway when an explosion ripped through the van's hood. The entire vehicle shuddered. Airbags inflated. Brakes squealed. The van veered to the left and began sliding down the street, until it crunched to a halt against a Yugo.

Almost instantly, two figures ripped the sliding door from its hinges hopped through the opening. They had long sharp fingernails, glowing red eyes and smelled of mold and decay.

The vampires quickly dispatched the pledged in the back seat. They tried to put up a fight, but their weapons did little to slow the assault. The front two died even quicker.

Ignoring her muffled screams, the vampires grabbed Penny and hopped away from the highway. Two seconds later, they dropped her at Chen Yung's feet.

The Petals had sent Chen Yung to capture Tondrell's Bar, a minor feng shui site in downtown Seattle. He had just arrived in the contemporary juncture when Bob intercepted him. Chen Yung knew Bob from an earlier mission, and after listening to his jumbled explanation, agreed to save Penny.

In return, Penny helped Chen Yung buy out the Tondrell's Bar, thus gaining the feng shui site without drawing unwanted attention. Noting her uncontrolled magical ability, Chen offered to take her back to the 69 juncture. There, she began learning the pathway to true power.

It did not take long for the Petals to realize Penny's potential. She had the knowledge and experience that they needed in the contemporary juncture. Unfortunately, we do not allow women into the Eaters of the Lotus, and no one would accept a non-member general. So they reached a compromise. Chen Yung became the contemporary general with Penny as his advisor. Of course, everyone knows that Penny holds the reigns. Chen Yung merely acts as a figurehead and teacher, an arrangement that suits him fine.

In the six months since she took control, Penny has established small Lotus outposts in Hong Kong, Tokyo, London, New York and San Francisco. She created a phony computer consultation firm, DataTel Inc., and uses their offices as a front for Lotus activity. The Petals insisted that she place her headquarters in Kowloon, despite the valley's generally bad feng shui. After all, Kowloon means nine dragons — and the nine inner members (including Gao) saw that as a positive omen.

Like Cha Tzu, Penny relies heavily on recruits from the local juncture. This includes a handful of wizard-wannabes, though most help comes from her brother Tieh. Tieh teaches martial arts in San Francisco. He is an accomplished Fu master and an important member of the local Triad. Through his contacts, Penny has met important Triad leaders across the globe. He also provides her with the assistance of his students and peers.

All of Penny's recruits are highly loyal to her and her brother. Unfortunately, the traditional sorcerers from the 69 juncture feel differently. They dislike taking orders from a woman, and they resent that a minor sorcerer — an apprentice really — should rise to such power.

Many, in their arrogance, refuse to contact Penny for further instructions or advice. They arrive in the future, confident of their abilities, and head straight out to achieve the Petals' goals. More often than not, they end up bleeding in a gutter, the mission in tatters. For her part, Penny just ignores them. The smart ones will learn — the others deserve their fate.

Also, do not mistake Penny's optimism and energy for bubbleheadedness or a lack of resolve. It's a mistake you will only make once. Penny considers every obstacle to be a challenge, and she is not shaken by defeat. Rather, she uses her quick wits and mental flexibility to find another route to her goal. She will try to protect those under her command — refusing to risk them unnecessarily. But when it comes down to it, she will do anything that is necessary. It is this combination of creativity and determination that makes her a very dangerous opponent.

Fortunately, Penny remains unquestioningly loyal to the Eaters of the Lotus. We have given her power and abilities she could only dream about — and she owes us her life. I know that she disagrees with some of Gao's practices, but not enough to challenge his will.

2056

If the contemporary juncture was difficult to infiltrate, 2056 has proven all but impossible. Our operatives faced similar problems with cultural differences and a lack of technological savvy; however, the 2056 juncture also adds a thick layer of paranoia. To successfully infiltrate the juncture, we need a dizzying number of ID cards and paperwork. Even then, our names, fingerprints, and DNA must be on file in the appropriate computers. Any deviation will be spotted, the operatives arrested and either brainwashed or executed.

So far, only the Movement of the Twined Snakes has proven successful. This project started simply enough. A shape-shifting demon would kill and replace one member of an Architect capture squad. Using the borrowed identity, it would slip through the Buro's checkpoints. These early replacements sought out information, then quickly returned to Lo-yang. Later ones targeted and attacked specific people. A few tried to establish a permanent position within the 2056 society. These attempts were universally short-lived — someone invariably noticed a change in behavior.

However, as time has gone on, the project has broadened its methods. Members of the Metal division soon realized that we could magically bind the Architect's abominations, using their own soldiers as spies. Possessing spirits also began to replace shape-shifting demons. Both of these methods are harder to detect. Our spies have full access to the old identity's memories, and the process makes only slight changes in their behavior patterns. Possessing spirits have an added advantage: they can shift hosts when necessary.

So far, the impish spirit Thousand Questions has had the most luck infiltrating 2056. During a firefight, he possessed the body of an injured Architect soldier. Burying himself deep within the soldier's mind, he rode unnoticed into the future. Once there, he began jumping from one body to another, until he found a suitable host, John Sanders. John is a middle manager in the Buro — high enough to have useful contacts, low enough to remain unnoticed by his supervisors. More importantly, John had no family ties and no friends outside limited office acquaintances.

Horned Demon X-125-A

Attributes: Bod 9, Chi 5, Mnd 5, Ref 8
Skills: Arcanowave Device 16, Creature Power 14, Guns 12, Info/Architects 8, Info/Lotus 8, Martial Arts 12
Arcanowave Schticks: Helix Ripper, Neural Stimulator, Wave Suppresser
Creature Powers: Abysmal Spines (+2 Dam), Armor (+4 Tgh), Burning Blood, Regeneration (1 wp/seq)
Base Damage: 15 (helix ripper), 12 (claws)

Using John's contacts, Thousand Questions began establishing temporary identities for other Lotus infiltrators. To avoid attracting attention, Thousand Questions kept John from doing anything suspicious. Rather, the spirit would temporarily jump to another host, made the appropriate entries into the Buro computers, arranged for the necessary IDs, then return to John. Of course, someone would eventually discover these false identities, but the Buro's paper trail led back to an innocent wage slave. They arrested the poor suspect as a Jammer conspirator, dragging him off in shackles. This had a useful secondary effect – the arrest sends waves of confusion and resentment through the wage slave's family.

All in all, Thousand Questions rather liked his job.

However, as the months stretched on, Thousand Questions began to balk at our requests. It outright refused to set up the assassination of Arnold Thompson – an influential PubOrd Lieutenant. This confused both the Petals and the Wood Division, until the feng shui professor Gong Suan examined the 2056 juncture's feng shui. The Architects maintained control over their juncture not through their military might (which is significant), but through the overwhelming weight of their feng shui. In fact, their feng shui will have a growing influence on any operatives that remain in the 2056 Juncture. Eventually everyone will grow loyal to the Architects, save for those few with innate resistance (such as the Jammers) who do not fall under Bonengel's will.

This bothered the Petals. Not because of Thousand Questions. We had already fed him false information, anticipating his betrayal. Rather, it puts yet another crimp into our expansion plans.

Horned Demon X-125-A represents one example of their new, long term approach. This demon originally served Shen Yo, but the Architects captured it during an early battle. Over time, they bound the demon into their service and grafted it with Arcanowave technology, making it a front line abomination.

On one of the demon's return trips to the 69 Juncture, the sorcerer Hoi Mao Qian defeated it, binding it once more into the Lotus's service. However, Hoi ordered it to remain with its unit and return to the 2056 juncture. Once there, it reported back on any important Architect activities. Horned Demon X-125-A performed this role for months, slowly gaining the trust of Hoi Mao Qian and the Inner Council. Soon, they began using X-125-A to sneak new operatives into 2056.

The operation is simple. X-125-A pretended to capture the Lotus operative, either a supernatural creature or a sorcerer. It then escorts them back to the 2056. Once there, the Lotus operative only needs to survive the Buro Reeducation Programs and feng shui influences long enough to escape and complete their mission. Not an easy task.

Fortunately, X-125-A spends so much time outside the 2056 juncture that the feng shui influence never truly affects him. After seven months of service, he remains loyal and useful. He has the best success record to date.

The Petals have also tried to infiltrate the Jammers. This is somewhat easier. The Jammers have largely retreated into the Netherworld, thus removing the complications created by Buro paranoia and Architect feng

Tim Gunner, sorcerous pyromaniac

Attributes: Bod 5, Chi 0 (Mag 6), Mnd 5, Ref 6
Skills: Gun 13, Martial Arts 12, Sabotage 13, Sorcery 14
Schticks: Blast (fire, lightning)
Unique Schtick
Blown Clear: When caught in an explosion, Tim can make a defensive Martial Arts roll +5 (1 shot cost, Difficulty 0). Subtract his outcome from the explosion's damage.
Base Damage: 6 (hands), 16 (blast)

shui. Unfortunately, the Jammers' strong anti-magic propaganda make them hard to corrupt. Tim Gunner, one of Penny's recruits, has had some luck. He was a hacker punk who dabbled in home-brew explosives before signing on with Penny. Since then, he has added magic to his bag of tricks.

Tim seems to understand the Jammers and has developed a strong bond with many of them. He has even convinced a few Jammers of magic's benefit — secretly and discreetly of course. There's nothing like a spell-wielding pyromaniac adrenaline junky to demonstrate the sheer destructive power of the Blast spell.

While Gao wants to see the Jammers destroyed, he is not above sucking information and maybe a few recruits out of them first.

Other Expansion Plans

With the successful reawakening of Kun Chau, the Petals have decided to bury other things for our future operatives to uncover. We have considered binding other spirits to land masses in future strategic sites, burying magical treasures and similar methods.

Unfortunately, when it comes down to actually preparing these time capsules, we have relatively few resources that we can spare; worse, the nature of chi flow is such that these

capsules can only be retreived and used in the junctures, not in the intervening years. Our attempts to have them used at other points in history failed.

Some of our future recruits have suggested that we bury magical bombs — Blast spells that will lay inert until they are exposed to renewed magical energies. Then they explode. That way, when the CDCA begins reintroducing magic to the world, they will find several unpleasant surprises waiting for them.

Unfortunately this plan has several drawbacks. First, there's no way to target the weapons. They could be set off centuries early by a struggling mystic. Or they could destroy a single, low-powered abomination, thus wasting time and effort on a meaningless kill. Most importantly, however, this plan depends on our eventual defeat. Gao will not support any plan that shows a lack of faith.

However, despite the many problems, our future operatives have found several ways to reclaim lost resources. Both Cha Tzu and Penny have hired teams of archeologists to uncover lost tombs and ancient battlegrounds. They do not limit their searches to old Lotus goods, but seek out magical artifacts from Egypt, South America, Europe and other parts of the world.

Once they uncover an artifact, our Metal division studies them, awakening their power. We then recycle them into the secret war. This has provided both the 1850 and contemporary junctures with several minor magical tools.

We have also heard rumors from various informants suggesting that the Buro has also begun digging up archeological sites. Unconfirmed reports claim that they have discovered the Tomb of Xian Wang. According to legend, Xian Wang was a powerful king from the Xia dynasty. During his reign, ten thousand demons served by his side, including the demon lord Chiu Szu. Upon Xian Wang's death, all of these were sealed in his tomb, to await the call of the king to come after.

Reportedly, the Buro cannot yet open the Tomb. Still, it presents a tempting prize for any Lotus sorcerers that might reach it. Of course, the Petals hesitate to send a team though. It could easily be a trap. But there are undoubtedly a few ambitious individuals willing to risk their lives for glory. Perhaps one day, that will be you.

A cold wind blew off of the Loess Plateau, filling the air with its thin, yellow dust. From the top of this hill, Fire Vassal Hoi Mao Qian could see Lo-yang stretched out before him. The faint lights from oil lamps flickered like stars, echoing the vast sky above. Moving silently, Hoi Mao lit his own fires. Four bright flames quickly consumed the straw offerings, while nine joss sticks filled the air with their sweet smoke. Dipping his brush in the life-blood of a child, he wrote the proper spell and then touched the paper to the flame. Hoi felt the chi swirl around him like a wind from hell. Then the ground began to boil. Cracks formed between the four fires, and sulfurous smoke poured from beneath the earth. Slowly, the smoke congealed into gray-red skin. A form emerged, standing nine feet tall, with broad, muscular shoulders. Long, curved horns jutted from its head. Stepping forward, the demon bowed. "Master, my name is Two Ox. I have come to serve." Hoi nodded, a faint smile on his lips.

CHAPTER 4

The Supernatural

Where are you child? I heard you enter. I can hear your breath, your heart beat. Ah, yes. Lurking by the door. Well, come in. Sit beside me. Don't worry, I won't hurt you. Not tonight at least.

So they finally sent you down to me, eh? They've probably already filled your head with politics and lies. Forget all that. This is the true heart of our order.

The air around us is thick with supernatural influences. Ogres wander mist-shrouded mountain paths, while ancient ginseng plants offer immortality to those who tame them. You can feel the touch of gods and spirits throughout everyday life. They cause all sickness and misfortune. They are also the fount of health and good luck.

Local Gods and Spirits

Gods come in a variety of shapes and sizes, from the Jade Emperor in heaven to a family's earth spirit. But remember: as their power increases, so does their responsibility. The average person does not appeal to the Jade Emperor. Think of it, would a farmer take his troubles to the Son of Heaven directly? No, they turn to local authorities — regional magistrates or the village head man. Similarly, they pray to local spirits, ancestors and specific gods.

Life & Death

The family link between the living and the dead can carry feng shui influences from beyond the grave. Provided these are properly prepared and maintained, the descendants receive minor benefits of positive feng shui attunement. However, if they become desecrated, the descendants might find themselves shackled with harmful feng shui, as they are effectively attuned to a negative site.

The imperial court frequently uses this link as a weapon. The first response to any rebellion includes breaking into the rebels' ancestors' tombs, scattering their contents and desecrating the graves. This both disheartens the rebels and ensures the eventual downfall of their family. The Lotus have perfected this method — using it to weaken their enemies throughout time.

The Basics of Worship

You undoubtedly know the specific rituals and beliefs followed in your own home village. However, I doubt you can see how they fit into the divine tapestry. True, each town, even each family, has their own methods of prayer, but we can draw a few general comments. Listen carefully. Belief is a powerful tool — and it can become a powerful weapon.

At the bottom of the divine ladder sit the Great Aunts and Great Uncles. These spirits typically inhabit trees, streams and other natural features. Though generally friendly, they quickly turn vindictive when insulted or

Spirits & Purification

As long as these spirits and gods are happy, the area under their protection remains free of evil spirits and harmful influences. This has the same effect as the purification spell. The priest's AV when originally blessing the region determines supernatural creatures' difficulty for entering. This purification remains until someone offends the spirits or a supernatural creature manages to muscle past. In either case, a priest must perform the proper atonements and blessings before the purification returns.

Supernatural Forces

The supernatural aspects of the 69 junctures provide a variety of creatures. Some will aid the characters. Others will try to cut out their hearts and possess their bodies.

The characters should also feel the strong pull of unseen forces. Blessings and curses may manifest in many ways — but they most typically influence the character's chi flow. The village shrine and their ancient oak are both feng shui sites. While their spirits remain happy, those attuned to the sites gain positive chi. However, should they grow angry, the chi becomes negative and harmful.

improperly cared for. Still, they watch over the people living near them. They keep evil spirits away and offer advice during times of crisis.

Each Great Aunt or Great Uncle has a special festival in its honor. On this day virgins offer sacrifices of fish, pork, chicken, candles and joss sticks.

The next rung consists of household gods. Each house has their private protectors. A pair of doorway gods keep the home secure from harmful spirits. An earth god maintains the health and fertility of the family. Finally, the kitchen god lurks in its private altar in the kitchen. For the most part, people ignore the kitchen god — until New Year's. Every New Year's he leaves his altar and reports to the heavenly court. There he describes the family's behavior. Because of this, many people coat their icon's lips with honey. That way everything he says will be sweet.

Each village also has an earth spirit — basically a larger version of the household's spirit. This one lives beneath the fields and controls the village's fertility and crop production. In our highly agricultural society, the village earth spirit frequently becomes the most powerful everyday influence.

Villages also sport a number of local gods. These frequently have a small shrine or temple — simple structures with no statues or images of the god. As with the household gods and the Great Aunts and Uncles, the local gods protect the village. Unlike the other spirits, each local god has an area of expertise.

Each local god has a large festival in his honor. These typically last two or three days, with great feasts, musical performances, dancing, juggling and acrobatic feats. Ritual sacrifices include fine food, drink, incense and grain. More importantly, however, these festivals give the villagers a chance to relax and celebrate. They are typically high holidays — key points in the local calendar.

Religion in the imperial court runs along similar lines to that in the countryside — it just operates higher up the ladder. The Emperor and the court priests appeal to the Jade Emperor directly, or at least to his trusted counselors. After all, the Son of Heaven remains responsible for maintaining the welfare of the Empire. In fact, most of the Emperor's duties are rituals to ensure our prosperity.

Vassals

Attributes: Bod 5, Chi 0, Mnd 5, Ref 5
Skills: Martial Arts 8
Base Damage: 9 (sword)

Hoi Mao Qian, Fire Thorn

Attributes: Bod 3 (Con 4, Tgh 5), Chi 2 (Mag 9, For 5), Mnd 7 (Int 9, Wil 8), Ref 7
Skills: Deceit 9, Detective 8, Info/Farming 11, Info/History 13, Info/Politics 13, Intimidation 9, Sorcery 18
Shticks: Blast (Chi, Disease, Fire, Ice, Transmutation), Divination, Influence, Movement, Summoning, Transmutation
Base Damage: 11 (blast), 4 (hand)
Notes: Mao is a typical sorcerous Thorn. He bound the demon Two Ox to him with the sacrifice of a street urchin. Two Ox has served loyally for the last five years, asking for no other payment. Whenever Mao appears, he has Two Ox at his side, and at least a half-dozen vassals.

Two Ox, bound demon

Attributes: Bod 10, Chi 0 (Mag 8), Mnd 4, Ref 8
Skills: Creature Power 15, Deceit 9, Drinking 15, Intimidation 9, Martial Arts 12
Shticks: Immune to normal bullets, Armor (+4 Tgh), Insubstantial, Regeneration (2 wp/seq)
Base Damage: 14 (sword)

The Jade Emperor and the Heavenly Court

The order of heaven closely follows that of our Empire — or perhaps our Empire is modeled after the heavens. In either case, the Jade Emperor sits atop a massive bureaucracy. He is responsible for ordering everything within the universe: ensuring that crops grow, rain falls, and wind blows. From the smallest grain of sand, to the largest mountain — everything falls under his control. Of course, he delegates most of the true work to various officers and magistrates. These, in turn, delegate responsibility ever further down the ladder. Most of the Jade Emperor's true work consists of consulting with advisors, writing imperial decrees, and judging the cases brought before him by various gods (and heroes brave and crafty enough to make the journey).

Also like the imperial court, the officers and magistrates frequently shift as various gods gain and lose favor. Gods who offend the Jade Emperor often find themselves exiled to earth. Some simply bide their time wandering the countryside. They know the imperial whim will change, and they will then return to their post. Others, however, hope to win the Jade Emperor's favor by performing good deeds. In fact, of the powerful deities, only these gods in exile take a direct hand in human affairs.

The exiled gods' desire to right wrongs and help the innocent frequently brings them into conflict with us. Fortunately, they are rare, and the Empire is large. Exiled gods favor the countryside, where our power remains relatively weak. No child, this is a blessing. An exiled god could easily destroy our power center here at Lo-yang — shattering the whole organization.

True, the exiled gods only posses a shadow of their former abilities, but that still makes them some of the most powerful beings on earth. They remain immortal and can grant the gift of immortality to their companions. Most weapons and magic bounce harmlessly off their skin. And, to make matters worse, they usually come from hero or warrior stock. The more bureaucratic divinity tend to while away their exile — treating it as a vacation of sorts. Also, maverick hero gods more-frequently attract imperial displeasure and hence end up walking the earth quite often.

Though we have only encountered two exiled gods, the experiences taught us not to oppose them. Instead, Gao wants us to quicken the god's return to heaven. Our operatives set up false quests for the god to perform, ensuring a glorious victory. Meanwhile, Gao hires priests to pray on the god's behalf — reporting his good deeds to the Jade Emperor. The quicker the god leaves earth, the sooner we can return to business as usual.

Eunuchs of Heaven

A few of the more-theological members of our order have hypothesized that, since the Court of Heaven resembles the earthly court in so many ways, it must also have eunuchs. These divine eunuchs undoubtedly hold the strings to real power, just as we do. A few members have, therefore, formed a small cult, adopting the Eunuchs of Heaven as their patron deities.

However, most Lotus members would rather summon up demons and issue commands, than abase themselves before any supernatural power. A few offer the occasional joss stick or bowl of rice, just in case. But even the devout worshippers have yet to receive any obvious benefits. Perhaps the Eunuchs of Heaven do not exist. Perhaps they simply wait for a larger bribe. Regardless, this lack of evidence has not shaken the believers' faith. Their cult continues its slow growth.

Demons and the Underworld

Just as life, the earth and Heaven are part of the Jade Emperor's bureaucracy, so too are death and the Underworld. The demons have no power of their own — even the Yama Kings obey the Jade Emperor's will.

The Underworld acts as a gathering point for all the souls of the dead. Once here, their Underworld guides lead them before a Demonic Judge (or the Yama Kings themselves if the person merits such an honor). The judge then decides the soul's fate. Souls of the worthy are reincarnated as human beings — their prosperity in the next life depends on their actions in the last. Some even become gods or achieve enlightenment.

Most evil souls must spend some time in the Underworld. The demonic caretakers throw them into the pool of boiling blood, cast them onto the mountain of swords, or subject them to any of a thousand different punishments. Some stay in the Underworld for a time before reincarnation — though their

In many ways, the people of first century China treat their gods as supernatural insurance agents. They pick them based on service and value — trying to gain the maximum benefit from the minimum commitment. When their fortunes turn sour, they frequently look for a new god — someone who will treat them better. They even try to fool their gods, and based on their reports, most gods seem easy to fool.

Of course, matters quickly become more serious when the spirits of the dead are involved. Ancestor worship is very important. This comes, in part, from filial piety. Just as a dutiful son must honor and respect his parents, he must also respect their parents' parents and all the ancestors that came before.

More importantly, however, they try to appease the dead because they don't want them to return. They need to coax these spirits into abandoning the world of the living and continuing their journey to the Underworld. With the Underworld the way it is, these spirits are understandably hesitant. Still, they cannot remain bound to their earthly lives and desires. Those that try soon become hungry ghosts, feeding off the living.

However, ensuring their passage to the Underworld is only the first step. Their descendants must continue to follow the proper rites and observances, or the ghost may come back mad. Sickness, madness, poverty, failure and misfortune are all gifts of the angry dead.

Because of this, the location of a family grave becomes very important. Even the poorest farmer will hire a fortune teller or feng shui professor before arranging a funeral. Based on this information, they prepare the proper rituals at the proper hour on the proper day. Reburials are common, especially when the spirits complain about their current placements. Furthermore, every household maintains an alter to their ancestors. Here joss sticks are burnt and candles are kept lit as continual offerings.

— Dr. John Haynes, Dragon Observer, Full-Contact Historian and High-Caliber Anthropologist

The farming village of Lu Mi has remained practically unchanged for several millennia. During the Warring States period, two great armies marched into Lu Mi's valley, facing off across the small village. The townsfolk knew that, regardless of who won, they would carry the greatest losses. Fields trampled, livestock scattered — they would be lucky to survive the winter. But no one dared oppose the great generals.

However, Hei Jing grew tired of his family's worry and complaints. A gnarled, wild-haired old man, he gathered together his old military sword, a broken and rusted blade, and marched out to face the first general. When the camp's guards stopped him, he shouted, "I am the general of the city Lu Mi. Listen carefully. I will allow you to retreat in peace. But if you are still here tomorrow night, an army of our ancestors will rise from the ground, killing you to a man. Your wars will not harm Lu Mi!"

The guards laughed and sent him back to the village. But that night, each had vivid dreams of screaming ghosts and shambling corpses, clawing at their bodies with fingers of ice — biting with rotten jaws. The next morning they reported both Hei Jing's threats and their dreams to their general. He had also seen the dream, and ordered the army to strike camp by noon.

Meanwhile, Hei Jing marched up to the other army and repeated his performance. Again, the guards laughed him away — though a little nervously as they eyed the strange activity in the enemy camp. That night, they too met dreams of ghosts and corpses. And the next day, they retreated.

Word of Hei Jing's bravery reached the Jade Emperor, and upon Hei Jing's death, the Emperor made him a god. Since that time he watches over Lu Mi as their patron of warfare and conflict.

— Dr. John Haynes, Dragon Observer, Full-Contact Historian and High-Caliber Anthropologist

next life is also unpleasant. They come back as an impoverished wretch, an animal or perhaps a demon. Others remain condemned forever.

Hero Gods in the Game

Hero gods nearly always have incredibly good fortune (For 10 or higher). They attempt the ridiculous, and nearly always succeed. Fate aligns itself so they come out on top, and look good while doing it. Their enemies accidentally run each other through with their swords or catch themselves in a crossfire. Opponents' chariots flip over during the chase scene. In other words, they are the ultimate action heroes.

Consider this carefully before introducing one into any story. Unhindered, their abilities will outshine the characters, relegating them to spear-carriers. Of course, these gods could have amnesia (and not know how to access their power), could be held prisoner, or be subject to a similar fate. Maybe the characters get blamed for the havoc that the god creates — or maybe the god mistakenly attacks the characters (and beats them unmercifully). Plot possibilities abound.

Of course, this is only a sampling of possible afterlives. Some spirits go to other worlds. Some cease to exist. The final resting place of the dead is only limited by the individual's belief, and by the creativity of their Demonic Judge.

In any case, the underworld remains an unpleasant place, even for the demons who serve there. It is a land of extremes, from fiery pits to plains of razor-sharp ice. Our demons have described mountains of bones, caverns of living flesh and other nightmarish landscapes.

Here, the strong always lord over the weak, and upsetting your superior results in brutal punishment. Over the millennia, they have raised the creation of pain and suffering to an art form. For many, their only joy comes from harming others — weather they rise to earth and torture the living, or simply wrongly persecute the dead souls in their care. Many demons torture souls as they escort them along the hallway of hells. Some deliberately place them in the wrong afterlife — reincarnating a worthy soul as a dog, or casually tossing it into the pit of choking and drowning for a few hundred years.

A few people have complained about these excesses — but their words fall on deaf ears. The Yama Kings seem hesitant to deprive their underlings of this sport. Still, heroes have managed to fight their way to Heaven and present themselves to the Jade Emperor himself. On these rare occasions, an imperial edict guaranteed that all wrongs are set right. Still, for every soul that escapes this game, ten thousand remain in agony.

It should also come as no surprise that many demons and condemned spirits wish to escape the Underworld. Several rise to the world of men — either sent by their masters, or summoned by sorcerers. While here, their Underworld bosses cannot directly influence them. They can easily slip the unholy reins, breaking any remaining bonds.

But this is a poor sort of freedom. Their masters in the Underworld might have difficulty regaining control, but they will not let their servants slip away. The escaping demon soon finds himself hounded by numerous spirits. He can delay his fate by hiding or seeking a

Shen Chang, exiled god

Attributes: Bod 12, Chi 8 (For 12), Mnd 10, Ref 9

Skills: Guns 20, Info/Tactics 12, Info/Supernatural Creatures 12, Info/Weapons 12, Martial Arts 26

Shticks: Will Not Die, Regeneration (4 wp/seq), Incredible Speed

Unique Schtick

Dodge Magic: Shen Chang can attempt to dodge any spell, Creature Power, or Arcanowave effect. He uses his Martial Arts as normal.

Base Damage: 15 (staff), 13 (hands)

Notes: The Jade Emperor exiled Shen Chang for brawling in the Celestial Throne Room. Since his return to earth, he has spent his time drinking rice wine by the keg, and looking for trouble. He is a good-hearted fellow, easily upset by the plight of others. When he runs into trouble, he usually tries to solve it — with repeated blows from his staff.

Early in their rule, every Emperor climbs Mount T'ai to make sacrifices of bulls, jade and gold. In this way, he insures his right to rule. Some will repeat this ritual during times of trouble.

In truth, Mount T'ai is a powerful feng shui site. When the Emperor makes his sacrifices, he attunes himself to it, becoming the channel for a vast river of positive chi. While the Emperor rules justly, the good chi flows through him, spreading out across the Empire. People live good lives. Their crops remain plentiful, and disasters rarely strike.

However, when he rules out of greed the flow stops, and the Emperor begins absorbing the chi directly. While this makes him immediately more powerful, it harms the land. Crops begin to fail. Natural disasters wipe out entire villages. People begin muttering that Heaven has withdrawn its mandate. The Emperor, heady with this new power, rarely sees this growing anger.

However, the Emperor's attunement to Mount T'ai depends on his service to the land. The longer he tries to hoard its power, the weaker his connection becomes. Eventually, his attunement dissolves, and his personal power disappears. This typically marks the beginning of open rebellion — possibly the end of a dynasty.

The Current Son of Heaven tries to rule justly, and heaven maintains its mandate. However, the Eaters of the Lotus have tapped into his connection. They draw off a measure of the Empire's positive chi. In this way, they grow strong at the Empire's expense.

So far, the effects are limited. Gao carefully controls the siphoning, taking only a small percentage of the Empire's allotment. He has read the historical records and understands the risk of abusing Mount T'ai. Still, while the small drain has a barely perceptible influence on the Empire, it represents a vast increase in power for the Lotus.

Ironically, as the Lotus expand this feng shui becomes diluted, encouraging Gao to draw even more. He also tends to dip heavily into the Empire's allotment during times of trouble. Though he backs off after the danger has passed, he always keeps a little more. If left unchecked, Gao's growing dependence on this power will lead to the Lotus's downfall.

— Dr. John Haynes, Dragon Observer, Full-Contact Historian and High-Caliber Anthropologist

> The poor fools. Look at them. Their orders, their arrogant demands. Can't they see that we only obey because it serves our own purposes? Hah! By the time they realize our true power, it will be too late. Every day they grow more dependent on us. Soon they will be our slaves.
>
> — *Two Ox, bound demon*

safe haven, but eventually someone will reach him, dragging him back to the Underworld. For most, the fear of eventual punishment keeps them from even attempting an escape.

However, a few turn their back on evil and pain, seeking redemption. After making his first few steps along the pathway toward enlightenment, their masters lose all claims. He is free to live his life on earth — unless condemned by further evil acts. Once he gives up his search for redemption, the old bonds return.

The most common (and most reliable) method of escape requires the demon to find a replacement. Their masters do not care who serves them. One soul is as good as the next. However, the conditions of this replacement seem to vary, depending on the master involved. Some will take any souls — the demon need only arrange a mortal's death. Others require the mortal to voluntarily exchange positions with the demon. Still, once the exchange takes place, the demon is free from all future obligations.

Drowned Ghosts

Sometimes a violent or horrific death will confuse the emerging ghost. The most famous example is the drowned ghost. He becomes lost, unable to find his way to the Underworld. Threatened with oblivion, he clings to his death. He becomes trapped.

Some gain control over the water which killed them. They can cause or prevent floods, control aquatic animals and such. Many fishermen pour out a glass of wine as an offering to drowned ghosts — hoping to receive a bountiful catch. Others begin to worship them as gods.

But despite this worship, the spirit cannot stray from the place where it drowned. It remains eternally shackled to that one spot of water. However, like the demons and spirits of the underworld, the ghost can transfer this bond to another. When another person drowns there, they become the ghost, and the current ghost goes free.

Because of this, most drowned ghosts become hostile. They cause people to trip while walking along the riverbank, or capsize boats out in the water. Some can even possess their victims, luring them to a watery death.

Of course, similar ghosts appear after other violent deaths. They are likewise tied to a spot, or sometimes an item. An assassinated ghost may haunt his killer's dagger — waiting for another to share his fate. This can create a cycle of murders. Once each new ghost gains a measure of power, they possess the dagger's current wielder and arrange for their replacement.

Hui Xue, drowned ghost

Attributes: Bod 7, Chi 0 (Mag 7), Mnd 5 (Cha 8), Ref 9

Skills: Creature Power 14, Martial Arts 10, Seduction 11, Sorcery 13

Creature Shticks: Body Borrow, Flight, Insubstantial, Regenerate (1 wp/seq)

Magic Shticks: Influence, Weather

Notes: At the age of 16, Hui Xue was walking home by the river's edge when she tripped and fell into its icy water. At that point, the drowned ghost previously trapped there was freed. Hui Xue took his place. Over the next fifty years, she has learned to tap into some of the powers at her control. She continues to try and lure victims into the water, but so far, she has had no success.

Inanimate Spirits

Sometimes the spirit of an object learns to take physical form. They emerge only at night, prowling around and haunting their surroundings. They seem universally malicious. Driven by inhuman hungers, some attack anyone they happen across. Others specifically hunt the person most associated with their daytime form.

Remember: the inanimate spirit's shape does not necessarily have any relation to their daytime form. Most take on monstrous bodies or resemble deformed animals.

No one knows why objects acquire inanimate spirits. Some emerge after witnessing violent emotions. Others, after simple years of daily use. Few sorcerers know the secret to waking an object's spirit — or making it sleep again.

Bowl Bird, inanimate spirit

Attributes: Body 5, Chi 0 (Mag 5), Mnd 4, Ref 7

Skills: Creature Power 12, Martial Arts 12

Shticks: Blood Drain (fortune drain), Flight

Base Damage: 9 (talons)

Maidens from Heaven

The daughters of the gods have magical clothing which allows them to assume the shape of birds. Using this form, they descend from heaven, bathe in mountain springs or pools, then fly back to their home in the sky. Groups of maidens typically have a favorite spot which they visit every few days.

While bathing, the maidens are vulnerable. Anyone can sneak up and steal their clothing, without which they cannot return to heaven. Several enterprising young men have used this trick to acquire divine beauties as their wives. When the men are good-hearted and decent, the maidens actually fall in love with them. In these cases, the clothing trick seems more like an introduction than actual kidnapping. On the other hand, unworthy husbands quickly find themselves abandoned. Regardless of how sneaky or deceptive he is, the maiden eventually outwits him. She regains her clothing, turns into a bird and flies back to heaven — usually leaving the poor man's life in disarray.

A few crafty heroes have also used this trick, not to gain a wife, but to grab the attention of the maiden's heavenly parents. He uses the kidnapped maiden to negotiate with the gods themselves, demanding their assistance. In this way, heroes have saved villages from drought or the ravages of war. They have chased evil spirits and demons from the countryside. One even had a god bring his wife back from the dead.

It is important to realize that this trick only works for people with good intentions. Mang Fu, one of our underlings, tried using it to gain support for his plots. The god in question quickly reduced Mang Fu to a pile of smoking ash, then created a new set of clothing for his daughter. The two returned to heaven unhindered.

Jin Tao, the wife of a wealthy farmer, suddenly became sick. She showed no signs of injury and had no symptoms, save a weariness that grew worse each day. By the end of a week, she could no longer rise from bed. Qaio, Jin's husband, called in a priest. He examined her at length but also found nothing.

That night the priest decided to keep watch. He sat outside Jin's door, waiting for something to happen. Sure enough, around four in the morning he heard a loud flapping inside the room.

The priest burst in, only to find a huge black bird resting on Jin's chest. It lowered its beak to her mouth and sucked the breath from her sleeping body. Then it noticed the priest. Rising into the air, it raked his face with long sharp talons. The priest simply lifted a blessed spell he had written for just this occasion. Magic burned into the bird. With a howl, it flew away.

The priest chased the bird into Jin's kitchen. Once there, the bird settled into a large wooden bowl — the bowl Jin used to mix bread dough. It slowly melted into the wood, disappearing completely. Without pausing, the priest set his spell into the bowl, then filled it with rocks and buried it in the farmer's field. That morning Jin recovered.

— Dr. John Haynes, Dragon Observer, Full-Contact Historian and High-Caliber Anthropologist

Immortality

Many sages have long sought the secrets to immortality. Some drink potions of mercury and toxic herbs, hoping to kill that which causes their body to decay. Others spend their days meditating, seeking eternal life through enlightenment. For some, gaining immortality is as simple as eating a peach, or the result of an unfortunate accident. A few extend their life through sleep.

Many pathways to immortality lie beyond the edge of the known world. Exploration parties search for the Eastern Isles of the Ocean to find the immortal beings living there. Others seek out the Queen Mother of the West, who confers the blessing of immortality to her pilgrims.

Don't get excited. Most of these quests fail. The seekers poison themselves, or waste

Whether individually or as a group, the Eight Immortals travel about China acting as teachers, advisors and priests. They avoid conflicts, but often take on students, teaching them magic, fu powers or supernatural abilities. These students have become some of the Lotus's worst enemies. A few have stepped fully into the secret war, joining the Dragons.

— Dr. John Haynes, Dragon Observer, Full-Contact Historian and High-Caliber Anthropologist

their life searching for mystical knowledge. An unfortunate few find everlasting life, but not what they wished for. They become undying corpses, or evil spirits preying on the chi of others. Very few actually succeed.

Over a hundred immortals or near-immortals walk the land. Of these, the most famous are the Eight Immortals — the Taoist paragons of true immortality and spiritual enlightenment. Despite their great power, they refuse to become involved in worldly affairs. Instead, they waste their time wandering aimlessly and writing poetry. Pay them no mind.

The Eight Immortals

Chung-li K'uan became the first true immortal. He discovered the elixir of life — a potion that grants both physical immortality and spiritual perfection to anyone drinking it. He also carries with him a fan that can revive the dead. Chung-li's symbol is the peach — also a symbol of longevity.

Chung Kwoh-Lao began his quest as a recluse and mystic. His studies gave him many magical powers and tools, including a mule which can travel a thousand miles in a day.

Chung Kwoh-Lao can fold this mule and stick it in his pocket. When he needs it, he simply sprinkles water on it. His symbols are a feather of the Phoenix, and a yu ku (a musical instrument made from bamboo).

Lu Tung-pin studied as a Taoist scholar and became a recluse. While following Chung-li K'uan he learned the secret of immortality. However, before becoming worthy of the gift, he had to undergo ten temptations. At the end of this testing, he was given a magical sword, which he used to rid the countryside of dragons and monsters. His symbols are the sword and the fly-brush.

Once a military commander, **Ts'ao Kuo-Chiu** turned his back on the material world and became a hermit. One day while meditating, the wall of his cave split open, revealing a casket of jade. Inside Ts'ao found a scrolls containing the secrets of immortality and of transmuting metals. As he followed the first scroll's instructions, the cave filled with a glowing cloud. Soon a giant stork appeared and carried Ts'ao to the Happy Land of Immortality. He has since become the patron of drama. His symbol is a feather fan.

Li Tieh-Kuai used to study under Lao Tzu. One day Lao summoned Li's spirit to heaven, instructing him to leave his body in the care of his best pupil. Unfortunately, during Li's journey, the pupil was called to the bedside of his dying mother. Other students found Li's body and thought him dead. Stricken with grief, they consigned the body to the flames.

When Li returned, he found only a pile of ashes remaining. Desperate, he entered the body of a beggar who had just died. He has spent the remaining years in that crippled body, hobbling around on a crutch.

Li's symbol is a pilgrim's gourd, which contains a powerful medicine. He frequently travels the world, healing the sick, and has become the patron of herbalists and doctors.

Han Hsang-Tzu studied under Lu Tung-Pin as scholar and poet. One day Lu instructed Han to climb a peach tree. As he approached the top, Han slipped, falling to the ground. He has been immortal ever since.

Han Shang-Tzu can make flowers grow and bloom as people watch. He is the patron of music, and his symbol is a flute. He spends most of his time entertaining: playing the flute, reciting poems, or simply opening people's minds to the wonders around them.

Lan Ts'ai-Ho spent her life as a strolling singer. Her songs spoke about the unreal, fleeting nature of life and the delusiveness of earthly pleasures. She always wore a blue robe and one shoe. When her earthly body died, she disappeared, rising into the clouds. Her symbol is a basket of flowers.

Ho Hsien-Ku, the Immortal Maiden, learned that eating only mother-of-pearl would gradually transmute her into an immortal. For years she kept to her strange diet. Gradually her body became lighter and more ethereal, until she could skip from peak to peak along the mountains. But she only became truly immortal after giving up on all earthly food. Her symbol is the lotus, the flower of open-heartedness.

If the Eight Immortals are the paragons of enlightened immortality, the Five That Will Not Die are icons of immortality gone wrong. These are the twisted, evil products of failed attempts at everlasting life. Technically they are not immortal — that implies a spiritual purification. They have simply gained longevity, albeit everlasting longevity.

— Dr. John Haynes, Dragon Observer, Full-Contact Historian and High-Caliber Anthropologist

The Five That Will Not Die

Less famous than the Eight Immortals — but more important — are the Five That Will Not Die. Study them carefully. While they wield great power, they represent the dangers inherent in the quest for everlasting life.

Two Axes

Five hundred years ago, Two Axes rose to power as a warlord along the northwestern frontier. He carved a kingdom out of the wind-swept grassland, leading an army that numbered in the thousands.

One day his guards captured a wagon containing crates of books, ingredients and alchemical tools. The only occupant was the wagon's driver, an old man dressed in simple hemp clothing. The guards brought the old man before Two Axes, accusing him of practicing sorcery. Just as Two Axes opened his mouth to condemn the old man, the sorcerer begged to speak with him — privately.

Nodding, Two Axes dismissed his guards, then leaned forward and listened to the old man's promise.

"I can give you immortality," the old man whispered. "I know the secrets of everlasting life. Let me live, let me leave your lands, and the secrets are yours."

Two Axes already felt the weight of his years. He longed to be young again, to have time to conquer all the world, not just a small, northern kingdom. He readily agreed to the old man's request.

That night the old man visited Two Axes' tent. He spread a reed mat, inscribed with a hundred spells. As Two Axes' head touched the mat, he could sense its magic wrapping around his body like a heavy wool blanket. The feeling in his arms and legs vanished. His sight dimmed, then only the regular thudding of his heart remained.

Using spells and surgery, the old sorcerer split open Two Axes' chest and removed his heart. He then sealed the still-beating organ in a clay jar, and inscribed the spell to protect it. With a clap of the sorcerer's hands, Two Axes awoke.

"You must protect this," he said, handing the heart to Two Axes. "As long as it remains intact, you cannot die. Any damage will heal within days. However, should the jar gain the slightest crack, death is instantaneous."

Since then, Two Axes has lived to see his kingdom destroyed. He traveled China as a mercenary, fighting for whomever could pay him. All the time, he carefully protected his heart.

However, the surgery has a slight side effect. Without his heart, Two Axes' emotions have muted. He lost his passion, but not his desires. Two Axes does not get angry, does not feel regret. He has grown cold and utterly ruthless.

Deng Mei

As a boy, Deng Mei apprenticed himself to the Taoist wizard Lei She. For a decade he studied, learning the names of every plant in the woods, and all the animals and birds as well. He observed the stars and their influence, the spirits and their moods. He learned minor spells and medicine. But he knew none of his master's true secrets.

Well into his eleventh year of study, Deng spent yet another day clambering across the mountain gathering herbs. Suddenly he stumbled upon a great ginseng plant. Over a thousand years old, the plant had gained a measure of intelligence. More importantly, it had grown into true power. Deng dug up the precious root, struggling as it tried to squirm from his fingers. Tying it tightly in his bag, he returned to his master's cave and presented it triumphantly.

Much to Deng's surprise, Lei knocked the ginseng root from his hands, and ordered

Two Axes

Attributes: Bod 8, Chi 0, Mnd 5, Ref 9

Skills: Guns 15, Info/Politics 12, Info/Tactics 15, Intimidation 15, Leadership 12, Martial Arts 22

Shticks: Regenerates (1 wp/seq), Will Not Die

Base Damage: 12 (sword)

Notes: If the jar containing his heart gets even the slightest crack, Two Axes will die. Needless to say, he tends to keep it hidden somewhere very, very safe.

Deng to return it to the ground. "Such spirits are not to be taken lightly. How dare you rip it from the ground without even the slightest ceremony. You are not ready to handle such powers."

Cowed, Deng gathered up the root and left his master's cave. He began climbing back down the mountain, but his master's words burned within him. After all these years of cleaning and back-breaking chores, how dare Lei She treat him so? Not ready? By his master's scale, he'd never be ready. Not for real magic.

Then another squirm of the root interrupted Deng's thoughts. Glancing into the bag to make sure it remained bound, Deng thought back to his studies. He knew about ginseng — not enough to unlock all of its powers, but enough. By rubbing its blood-like sap on his

Deng Mei

Attributes: Bod 12, Chi 0 (mag 6), Mnd 5, Ref 8

Skills: Info/Supernatural Creatures 15, Martial Arts 15, Medicine 18, Sorcery 22

Sorcery Shticks: Blast (Acid, Chi, Fire, Lightning, Magical Disruption), Divination, Heal, Move, Summoning, Transmutation

Base Damage: 13 (hands), 8 (blast)

feet he could walk on water. Ingested, a bit of the root would heal any illness or injury. With proper care, he could keep it alive and growing indefinitely. If he was careful and rationed it well, he would never grow old, never die. His bag held more power than his master ever offered him — than his master ever would offer.

In that instant, he made his decision. Instead of returning the root to the ground, Deng climbed down the mountain to the city of Lu'hou. Acting as a healer, he sold ginseng slivers to the sick and dying. That money bought him a wardrobe of ice-white silk, several horses, a carriage and a sturdy iron cage. Keeping the root locked in the iron cage, Deng traveled throughout the Empire. Every day, he cut off and ate a thin slice of the root. He studied under any scholars or sorcerers he could find. And, whenever his money ran low, he took on the role of doctor — his miracle touch healing patients that others had abandoned.

So things continued for another ten years. Deng's fame grew. The best teachers in the land gladly accepted him as a student. He even had students begging to study with him. He mastered many arts of magic and medicine, and soon only rarely resorted to the root to heal others. But every day he cut off another sliver for himself.

Unfortunately, his body began to attune itself to the root. As his knife sliced through its flesh, he could hear its screams echoing in his mind. Within another ten years, its whimpers began keeping Deng awake at night. Soon he could feel the root's pain as the knife cut into it. These distractions grew so extreme that Deng retreated from the world, hiding in a cave much like Lei She's.

Centuries passed, wrapped in screaming pain and howls of anger. Deng now feels every second of the slow torture he inflicts on the root. But he cannot give it up. His body looks fitter than an athletic eighteen year old's. He has the strength of five men, the reflexes of a cat. He knows most of the universe's secrets. But his soul has grown hard, twisted and evil. He has become anger incarnate, striking out at any he can find.

Misfortune's Daughter

Misfortune's Daughter was born to poor rice farmers in the south reaches of the Empire. Of course, that is not her real name, but rather a name she adopted one thousand years ago. She no longer remembers her real name — just one of many things lost during her life.

She was just a girl when the raiders attacked her village. She remembers her parents standing at the window, bows in hand. Then a bandit broke into the hut, cutting them both down. He scooped up Misfortune and rode into the night. For a week, she lived shackled to the back of a long rope of slaves. Eventually, they reached a port town on the coast of the South China Sea.

There, a young man who smelled of sharp bitter herbs bought her. He forced her to drink a potion that smelled like rusting metal and rotten meat. Too scared to resist, Misfortune swallowed the foul mix. Almost immediately, pains stabbed at her stomach, then spread out into her arms, legs and head. For nearly two days, she could do nothing but lie in a ball and scream. Then the pain subsided.

The young man seemed pleased. He presented Misfortune with a feast greater than any she had ever seen. But when the first bite of food hit her stomach, the pains returned, and Misfortune retched until her body lay empty again. A few days later, patches of mold began to grow on her skin. Within a month, the rotting remains of her flesh hung to her skeleton like rags. The young man seemed quite upset.

One night he took Misfortune out on a boat. Once there, he tied a large bag of stones to her legs then pushed both overboard. She sank to the bottom — but did not die. After several hours of struggling, she untied her legs. It took two more days to walk to shore. She then escaped into the wilderness, to live as best she could.

Centuries passed but Misfortune never changed. Her body became that of a corpse — like the walking corpses a sorcerer might summon, except she still had her mind. Periodically, she grew lonely and tried to seek out companionship. Of course, everyone who saw her fled in terror. Even animals shied away. Only the scavengers seemed interested, and they just wanted to peck at her flesh.

Misfortune's Daughter

Attributes: Bod 8, Chi 0, Mnd 5, Ref 12
Skills: Intimidation 12, Martial Arts 19
Creature Shticks: Abysmal Spines (+ 6 dam), Regenerates (4 wp/seq), Will Not Die
Base Damage: 14 (claws)
Notes: Misfortune's Daughter and her Hands practice a form of martial arts called Corpse Fu. It is a frightening though otherwise unspectacular art form. They make an Intimidation check when attacking a new opponent (no Shot cost); the difficulty is the opponent's Willpower. Subtract the outcome from their opponent's remaining shots. This only works the first time someone faces Corpse Fu. After that, they are immune.

Misfortune's Hands, unnamed bandits

Attributes: Bod 5, Chi 0, Mnd 5, Ref 6
Skills: Intimidation 8, Martial Arts 8

She did not need to sleep or eat or breathe. Her body repaired any new damage — but would not grow or heal from its corpse-like condition. She remained trapped in the perpetually-rotting, eight-year-old body.

Eventually she gave up on friendships and simply lurked around the outskirts of temples, villages and cities. She studied people, watching the way they interacted, trying to emulate the things they did. She learned many skills, hiding near them. She learned more by watching animals in the wild, and by listening to the world around her.

One day she realized that the young man who had bought her was an alchemist, and that she was the result of a failed experiment. This sprung a new hope in Misfortune. If an alchemist created her, perhaps one could turn her back to normal. She began to search for other alchemists, then visited them in secret. Most sent her away, terrified of her visage. But one invited her in.

Even he did not treat her like a person. She was a specimen. He would occasionally cut a small bit off her finger, or remove a sample from her arm. He ran numerous tests. But after a year, he had come no closer to finding a cure.

One night, Misfortune grew angry, as he cut yet another slice of skin from her arm. She lashed out at him, her bony hand ripping through his flesh like a claw. His cries filled the night, and she ran out into the street.

People screamed as they saw her, and soon a group of guards approached, swords in hand. Using movements she had copied from monks and wild beasts, Misfortune launched herself at the guards, clawing and gouging a path through them. Everyone fled, leaving four dead bodies at her feet.

Something inside Misfortune changed. She was tired of letting the world take things from her. She was tired of watching others, knowing she would never be like them. From that day on, she strode proudly into villages and cities, taking what she wanted and killing any who tried to stop her.

Her reputation spread, and she soon found a number of bandits eager to join her. They treated her with respect, teaching what they knew, while learning from her experiences. She now commands a band of five hundred. Before each raid, the bandits paint their skin white, darkening their eye sockets and fingernails. Their favored weapon is a set of iron claws worn on both hands.

Kuei Chih and Thunder Under Mountains

The demon lord Thunder Under Mountains controlled a full province in the Underworld. With one command he could condemn ten thousand souls to the pits of scalding air. Another could redeem them, allowing all to pass to the next life. For nearly one thousand years, he was law, and he lived well — or as well as anyone can there.

But Thunder Under Mountains grew greedy. He watched the Yama Kings with an envious eye, and plotted his own rise to power. He told no one, fearing that they might find out. Instead he brooded in silence.

However, Thunder had one weakness. He loved alcohol, and readily drank to excess. So, one day Five Claws of Anger brought him ten kegs of rice wine as a tribute. That night, they opened the first barrel, and by morning not one drop remained. Thunder drank most of it.

His tongue loosened by the drink, Thunder told Five Claws about his plan to rise above the Yama Kings. With badly slurred words, he described his hidden stores of weapons, and the demons loyal to his command. He explained how his province would rise up. How he would soon lead an army of demons and condemned souls against the Hall of Judgment. He would cast the Yama Kings out and rule it all.

Five Claws had long suffered under Thunder. He brought the alcohol, hoping it would reveal something incriminating, and was not disappointed. As soon as Thunder fell asleep, Five Claws raced to the Hall of Judgment and repeated every word. The Yama Kings had Thunder brought before them. As he stood there, still swaying from the drink, they condemned him and cast him from the Underworld. He would become a hungry spirit, roaming the earth for eternity. In an instant he raced toward the surface, naked without a real body. About to abandon himself to misery, he caught a whiff of his favorite scent.

Kuei Chih, the village drunk, was fishing and drinking plum wine from a gourd when he heard the ground rumble. A hot breeze whipped around him, and the air filled with the screams of ten thousand souls. Suddenly a spirit appeared. It stood fifteen feet tall, its well-sculpted muscles rippling with each movement. The creature's skin looked jet black, as if charred in a hot fire. Two ox-like horns rose from either side of its head, and numerous spines sprouted from its back, shoulders, elbows and knees.

Paralyzed with fear, Kuei Chih watched as the spirit reached toward his wine. But the six-inch claws passed through the gourd — they were no more solid than an early-morning fog. Howling with anger, the spirit leapt at Kuei Chih, and their bodies collided. The demon's form disappeared into his own.

Kuei Chih

Attributes: Bod 5, Chi 0, Mnd 5, Ref 5
Skills: Drinking 8, Info/Farming 8, Info/Fishing 8
Creature Shticks: Will Not Die
Base Damage: 6 (hands)

Thunder Under Mountains

Attributes: Bod 8, Chi 5, Mnd 6, Ref 7
Skills: Creature Powers 16, Drinking 15, Martial Arts 18
Creature Shticks: Blast (fire), Conditional Escalation (+1 Bod when he takes more than 10 wp from a single attack), Regeneration (3 wp/seq), Will Not Die
Base Damage: 18 (blast), 9 (hands)
Note: These are the relative abilities, depending on which spirit currently controls the body.

The resulting possession was more accident than intent. Kuei Chih was using his body at the time, and Thunder Under Mountains did not have the strength to drive him out. So, for one hundred and fifty years they have shared control, the demon's spirit preventing any further aging.

Only one spirit can control the body at a time — and there is a marked difference in personalities. Kuei is a friendly, jovial man. He enjoys laughter and relaxing by the riverside. On the other hand, Thunder is loud, angry and insulting. He believes himself superior to the mortals around him, issuing orders like a king. Unfortunately, when his wishes aren't met he begins to smash things.

Despite the worn and weary body he now inhabits, Thunder Under Mountains can still smash with the best. While he controls the body, it gains unnatural strength. He can also tap into a smattering of his previous powers, giving him a selection of supernatural abilities.

The controlling spirit can block out the other, reducing it to a faint voice in the back of his head. This control usually lasts until he falls asleep or drinks himself into oblivion, though Kuei sometimes relinquishes control during times of danger, unleashing Thunder Under Mountains on a would-be attacker.

Still, Kuei hates Thunder Under Mountains. He feels guilty for the demon's actions, and tries to atone as best he can. At times he goes for weeks without sleep, just to keep the demon under control. Other times he drinks until his mind goes numb — hoping he will not remember the nightmare that follows.

For his part, Thunder seems to relish taunting Kuei. He commits atrocity after atrocity, knowing how Kuei suffers. After a millennia torturing others, some habits are hard to break.

Luan Ou

Dead body chi, as its name suggests, is the chi that gathers in bodies of the dead. Most of the time, this chi harms the living. It blocks their normal, healthy chi and creates illness and pain. For this reason, people avoid handling dead bodies.

However, Luan Ou became fascinated with dead body chi during his early studies of alchemy. As he watched healthy chi transform at the moment of death, he wondered if the process was reversible. If so, he could cure death — or at least prevent it. For a decade Luan Ou experimented on transforming dead body chi, all the while absorbing more of it into his system. Soon his own health suffered. Knots of pain formed in his back. His vision blurred, and he coughed constantly.

Finally, near death from exhaustion and illness, Luan Ou discovered the secret. He creat-

Luan Ou

Attributes: Bod 5, Chi 0 (mag 7), Mnd 6, Ref 5
Skills: Creature Power 18, Martial Arts 16, Medicine 20, Sorcery 14
Sorcery Shticks: Heal
Creature Shticks: Blast (chi), Damage Transfer, Will Not Die.
Unique Schtick
Infect Others: By slowly feeding a victim his dead body Chi, he can infect them with his dependence. They also gain the ability Will Not Die — and will slowly acquire his other abilities.
Base Damage: 9 (sword)
Notes: Luan must regularly eat fresh corpses to absorb their dead body chi.

Luan Ghouls, unnamed assistants

Attributes: Bod 5, Chi 0, Mnd 5, Ref 5
Skills: Martial Arts 12
Shticks: Will Not Die
Base Damage: 9 (sword)

In the past, the Five That Would Not Die rarely contacted each other. Each hungered for power, and their driving goals inevitably led to conflict. Contact with the Lotus went even worse. Over-eager sorcerers often tried to bind them. Some succeeded for a while, but the immortal's vengeance came quick and final.

But that was before the Secret War.

The eventual disappearance of magic has given them reason to cooperate. They all depend on magic for survival. Should it fade, their immortality will vanish and they will die.

The Five agreed to set aside their differences. They then approached the Eaters of the Lotus, offering to help. The Lotus represents their best chance for long-term survival. This creates a powerful and dangerous alliance.

Remember, however, that their relationship is based on pure self interest. As soon as this threat passes, they will begin fighting again. More importantly, once they can guarantee their survival without Lotus assistance, they will abandon the sorcerers.

— Dr. John Haynes, Dragon Observer, Full-Contact Historian and High-Caliber Anthropologist

ed a potion that forced the body to convert dead chi into healthy chi. Upon drinking it, he collapsed into a deep sleep. Three days later he woke, feeling fit and healthy once more. All the dead body chi was gone.

Months later, Luan Ou discovered that his secret had a price. His body now reclaimed dead body chi, but it refused to absorb any other type. At first this presented a minor inconvenience. Luan periodically handled dead bodies to top off his chi supply. But, as the decades passed, his hunger grew.

Now, four hundred and fifty years old, Luan Ou's body no longer converts dead body chi, but lives off it. He must eat fresh corpses to keep himself alive. Reduced to a wraith-like figure, he lurks along battlefields or graveyards. He robs family tombs, leaving the wealth untouched, but stealing the bodies. Doing so, he severs the family's ties to their ancestors, and condemns them to a slow decline.

His condition is also contagious. By touching someone, Luan can transfer the dead body chi stored within him. At this level of concentration, quick blasts of chi cause extreme pain, paralysis and even death. However, if transferred over several hours, the victim's body will become accustomed to it — and gain Luan's dependence. Luan occasionally uses this to make ghouls for his own protection.

Gaining Immortality

In general, immortals should be limited to GMCs — either allies who will teach the players the skills and abilities they need, or enemies for them to oppose. The quest for immortality lies outside the scope of these rules. Oh, it would make an interesting goal. After many sessions of appropriate roleplaying, the character might even succeed. But you should arrange the process between GM and player. It should depend on roleplaying and story, not artificial mechanics.

But wait, there's more. Before you decide to make your character immortal, remember: immortality is not easily gained. Only a minute percentage of the seekers actually find anything. Most of those find a false path. The road to everlasting life is riddled with the dead, cursed, damned and insane. You have been warned.

From a gaming context, immortality offers a lot of power. An immortal character could quickly overshadow the others — or simply defeat his opponents without any real challenge. For this reason, it is probably best if anyone gaining immortality retires from the secret war. He should follow in the footsteps of the Eight — teaching and advising heroes, but not entering the fight themselves. The immortal's player hands her character over to the GM and creates a new one — perhaps a relative or student of the new immortal.

Dragons

In the days of myth and legend, dragons freely roamed the land. Their strength was unequaled by any but gods and demons. But as magic began to ebb, they found themselves trapped in small, remote areas where magic was still strong: magic lakes, rivers or valleys.

These are, of course, the bearded dragons, often described as having a camel's head, a snake's body, lion's claws and carp's scales — though a few resemble giant turtles. Unlike their western counterparts, they do not have wings. Many can fly, but they prefer to swim. Also, they tend to breathe clouds of poisonous gas, not fire.

Dragons either protect an important body of water or control their region's rainfall. Most lakes and rivers have a resident dragon. Larger or spiritually-important ones will support a dragon court — a king or emperor ruling over several officers and subjects.

Rainmaking dragons, on the other hand, live away from water, usually in hidden valleys. These dragons fly through the sky, either by their own power or by adopting human form and riding magical steeds. By spraying drops of water into the sky, they crate rain. The method varies somewhat, but generally, one drop of water produces one foot of rain.

Most dragons can shape-change into a human form for a limited amount of time. This is their preferred form on land, letting them interact directly with the human world. Of course, most dragons can only reach communities that lie along their shores, and few have reason to do so.

Still, some acquired a taste for beauty. They trade pearls and undersea magic for items found only on land: gold and jade jewelry, silk garments and such. A few fall in love with particularly attractive mortals. After winning their desired marriage, they bring the new spouse to their kingdom beneath the waves. Humans brought to the dragon's court find that they can breathe as easily as on shore; however, they cannot leave without assistance.

Long Ti, imperial dragon

Attributes: Body 14, Chi 10, Mnd 8, Ref 10
Skills: Creature Power 15, Leadership 12, Martial Arts 20, Sorcery 15
Sorcery Shticks: Animalism, Blast (earthquake wave, lightning, water, wind), Divination, Fertility, Heal, Transformation, Weather
Creature Shticks: Abysmal Spines (+ 6 unarmed damage), Amphibian, Armor (+8 to Tgh), Burrowing (leaves tunnels), Enveloping Attack (2 shticks)
Base Damage: 20 (bite), 12 (blast)
Notes: Long Ti sits as Emperor over the dragons of Tian Lake. He knows that he can no longer leave the lake and its environs without turning human; however, he does not see that as a problem. The surface world holds nothing of interest — nothing compared to his empire beneath the waves.

So he sits contentedly, ruling over the dozen remaining dragons. Even the rebellious youngsters cannot keep him angry for long. Life goes on. Times change. But his empire is eternal.

Chung, dragon hunter

Attributes: Body 10, Chi 8, Mnd 9, Ref 12
Skills: Intimidation 15, Intrusion 12, Martial Arts 20, Sorcery 16
Sorcery Shticks: Blast (fire, water, wind), Movement, Weather
Fu Shticks: Bite of the Dragon, Breath of the Dragon, Claw of the Dragon, Natural Order, Backlash of the Turtle, Mirror of the Turtle, Laughter of the Turtle, Vengeance of the Turtle.
Base Damage: 10 (blast), 13 (sword), 12 (fist)
Notes: As the rebellion of younger dragons spread, a few of the loyal chose to take the fight to them. Long Chung is one of these. He abandoned his dragon form to hunt and kill any rebel dragons he can find.

He also works to increase the magic of the land — though he knows that will end with his own death. Note that Long Chung gains a Reversion point whenever he uses his Sorcery skill.

Long Kai, rebel dragon

Attributes: Bod 9, Chi 4 (For 8), Mnd 9, Ref 9

Skills: Intimidation 12, Leadership 10, Martial Arts 19

Transformed Animal Shticks: Bite of the Dragon, Breath of the Dragon, Claws of the Dragon

Base Damage: 11 (bite, claws)

Notes: Long Kai saw disaster on the horizon. The magic has steadily dropped since the age of legend. Soon, he and his fellow dragons found themselves trapped in their lake — unable to leave in their normal shape.

For years, Long Kai argued in the Imperial Court of the dragons. He tried to warn his brothers of their impending doom, urging them on to action. But the Imperial Dragon would not hear about it. He silenced Long Kai, and refused to discuss the matter.

Adopting human form, Long Kai left the lake and joined the world of mortals. It was an act of high treason, a slap in the Imperial Dragon's face. But he could no longer sit by and wither away.

Reveling in his newfound freedom, Long Kai roamed throughout all of China. He hired himself out as a mercenary and fought in a number of small wars. Soon, however, he realized that magic, once his ally, had become his enemy.

Long Kai had acquired the curse of all transformed animals — only worse. If he reverts, he will die. Since then, Long Kai has worked to further drive magic from the land.

Whether in their own form or in their mortal shape, dragons are fierce warriors. Many have also mastered the secret arts, particularly weather and sea magic. Fortunately, they cannot reach beyond their homes. As long as we leave them alone, they leave us alone.

A few unfortunate Lotus members have tried to grasp the treasures hidden under the waves. Others have harassed a person or village under a dragon's protection. The particularly-foolish even tried to magically bind a dragon. The result always ends in bloodshed — and the dragon isn't the one bleeding.

Best not to meddle in their affairs.

Dragons in the Game

Dragons cannot survive in areas with a Sorcery AV of less than +4. Since even the 69 juncture has dropped to +2, they remain trapped in small pockets of sorcerous energy.

However, there is a way out. When in human form, the dragons can easily travel from their magical prisons. Once outside the bubble of magic, they are then bound by all the rules and restrictions of transformed animals. However, if they remain outside for more than a month, they can never go back.

Many of the younger, free-thinking dragons gladly give up their reptilian form for freedom. They rebelled against their older, traditional brethren. Turning their back on magic, they seek to protect themselves in their new life. They look for places where magic will not touch them.

Though originally a string of isolated individuals, these rebellious dragons have begun to forge links with like-minded individuals — other dragons and transformed animals. After centuries of growth and development, this loose organization will grow into the Ascended.

For their part, the elder dragons mourn the loss of their own freedom — but they have never had more than a passing interest in the surface world. Blinded by tradition and inflexibility, they cannot see their doom approaching. As the magic continues to fade, their bubbles will pop. They will die.

A few realize that their younger brethren intend to drive magic from the land. This changes their actions from minor rebellion to outright treason. Forced to respond, the elder dragons send legions of human servants to capture or kill the young rebels. Some even abandoned their reptilian form to hunt these traitors personally.

Magic

The people in our land have a strange relationship with the magic around them. In many ways, magic is a part of everyday life. Farmers use rituals to ensure their crop's fertility. They cast small spells to heal the sick or protect their family.

On the other hand, most people fear magic. They respect the power of spirits and other supernatural creatures, but do not wish to interact directly with that power. Instead, they hire professionals: priests, fortune-tellers or mediums.

This suspicion of magic has even spread to the imperial court. Edicts have declared certain types of magic illegal, punishable by death. These include manipulating others or consorting with demons. Laws also prohibit animals from taking human forms — these abominations are hunted and killed upon discovery.

Ironically, Gao has encouraged these laws. It provides us with a useful mechanism for disposing of both enemies and unruly underlings — frame the victim for sorcerous crimes, and the guards take care of the rest. The heightened paranoia about magic also makes it difficult for rival secret societies to gain a foothold.

Still, there are several varieties of mystics and sorcerers that live and prosper throughout the Empire.

Mediums

Mediums are the most common mystics. These individuals allow various spirits to possess them. They give the spirits a voice, letting them talk to the living. Mediums frequently live in a temple, offering their services for a small donation. Most mediums cannot use their abilities to gain wealth or power — doing so would upset the spirits.

People frequently consult mediums when they are having problems. If the problems have a supernatural cause (an upset ancestor or angered spirit), the medium can then rec-

Mo Tsou, medium

Attributes: Bod 5, Chi 3 (Mag 8), Mnd 5, Ref 5
Skills: Info/Spirits 8, Medicine 8, Sorcery 14
Sorcery Shticks: Create Magical Artifact, Divination
Unique Schtick
Protected by Ancestor Spirits: Mo Tsou can dodge at her Sorcery AV +2 (16) even without the Blast schtick.
Base Damage: 6 (hand)
Notes: Mo lives deep in the woods, in a small hut beside a tiny lake. All the locals know the place, but no one goes there — not unless they need help. She tries not to let their ostracism bother her, since anger only interferes with her work. She eagerly provides advice, healing and good luck charms to any who ask.

ommend a solution — usually placating the spirit.

Most mediums work with a variety of wandering spirits, channeling those related to the issue at hand. A few, however, act as the mouthpiece for a single, more-powerful being. These beings typically come from the middle ranges of the supernatural hierarchy — powerful enough to have some influence, yet without overwhelming responsibilities. These range from local gods — whose medium serves as their temple — to powerful spirits of the land. In any case, the spirit in question has a vested interest in helping the local people. Their medium acts as his mouth and ears, answering questions and giving advice.

Mediums live a hard life, and few people choose it. Instead, the spirits call them. This typically happens at a young age. The medium's awareness to the supernatural awakens during their early teens. Accidents or severe illnesses can also trigger this awareness. Most mediums have yin eyes, or eyes of darkness. This allows them to see ghosts and spirits. Since yin (the female) is frequently associated with the supernatural, most mediums are women.

If they refuse the call or later abandon the spirits, the mediums inevitably suffer from continual illnesses and minor accidents. However, even faithful mediums seem condemned to short lives — though the spirits can delay death as a reward for selfless service. There are other dangers as well. While opening themselves to the spirits, the medium risks possession. Evil spirits can enter their body and then refuse to relinquish control.

Finally, the medium constantly lives on the edge of desire and hatred. Most villages depend on a medium for their livelihood. Still, their fear of the supernatural causes them to ostracize the spirit's servant.

A medium's duties include speaking with spirits, arranging passage to the underworld, sending gifts to spirits and arranging ghost marriages. They may also tell fortunes, create good luck charms and remove spells or evil influence.

Many spirits become lost on their way to the underworld. If these spirits remain bound to earth for too long, they become hungry ghosts, feeding off the living. However, mediums can ease their passage, creating a metaphysical passport for them. The medium writes an ornate document, then burns it — usually offering gifts as well. Though this helps the spirit find the underworld, it cannot force them to leave. The medium acts as a servant, not a master.

Mediums also arrange gifts for spirits. They make clay replicas for the family tombs, or burn straw and paper offerings. These gifts provide the spirit with the object in question. Mediums also use rice and joss sticks when working with spirits. Other offerings include food and wine.

Finally, their most unusual duty is undoubtedly the arrangement of ghost marriages. Here the medium oversees the wedding of dead spirits — typically spirits of infants and young children. After growing up in the underworld, these spirits find a desirable partner. Both spirits visit their parents during their dreams. They tell their parents about their wish to marry, and give them the name of their future spouse's family. The families then approach a medium, who performs the appropriate ceremony.

Occasionally, the spirits seek a marriage not because they have found a partner, but because tradition insists that they wed before a younger, still-living brother or sister. In these cases, the medium must also find an appropriate spouse for the spirit. Other times, the spirit cannot reach into its parents dreams and will find someone else to carry its message. In these cases, the medium must convince the parents, along with any other duties.

Healers, fu kay masters and fortune stick readers are all specialized types of mediums; they are described in the following sections.

Healers

Healers specialize in curing illnesses, particularly those caused by supernatural beings. They have a strong knowledge of medicine and herbs, matched with the abilities of a medium. They also know how to break evil influences and remove possession.

Healers treat both the mundane symptoms and the supernatural causes of the disease. They are the most frequently-visited mystic.

Fu Kay

This fortune-telling technique is a form of automatic writing. Here the medium balances a T-shaped stylus on his index fingers. As he enters a light trance, the stick begins to rock back and forth, sometimes becoming so violent that the fu kay artist must hold it with his thumbs. By lowering this stick into a box filled with sand, the fu kay artist begins to write mystical symbols. An assistant transcribes each of these. The artist then deciphers them with the help of a large dictionary.

In this way, the fu kay artist can receive answers to specific questions. As with all types of divination, these answers are typically cryptic or filled with riddles and mystic symbolism. Part of the fu kay artist's skill involves filtering relevant information from these predictions.

Many people feel that the answers from fu kay come directly from Lao Tzu, which would explain their frequently-sardonic nature.

Fortune Stick Readers

These mediums always work in a temple. Here the person seeking information shakes a large bundle of fortune sticks until one falls out. They then take that stick to the fortune stick reader, who interprets it for them. Each stick has a specific definition recorded in a large book at the temple; however, the definition is not enough to predict the seeker's fortune. The same stick could mean vastly different things to two different seekers. Therefore the fortune stick reader also looks at the supernatural influences surrounding the issue and then offers her advice.

Other Methods of Fortune-Telling

Other mediums decipher the cracks in burnt tortoise shells (similar to fu kay), or draw yarrow sticks to predict the future. For example, yarrow sticks are used with the I Ching, in a similar style to fortune stick reading. Both tortoise shells and yarrow sticks remain popular with the imperial court, and thus with wealthy merchants and land owners. Though they can be attempted by anyone, accuracy requires the assistance of a medium and help from spirits.

On the other hand, many people use palmistry and physiognomy to determine someone's inner character. Here the fortune teller examines the eyes, face and hands. The examination follows scientific principles and exact calculations. For that reason, it does not rely on spirits. This frees its practitioners from the curse of mediumship — also allowing them to charge outrageous fees for their services.

Bone reading is a similar skill. Here the practitioner feels the arm bones of an individual. Typically practiced by the blind, this has a more mystical nature than simple palmistry. The blind are believed to have a strong connection with the supernatural, and many are mediums.

Astrology and Numerology

Based on the position of the planets and the stars, astrologers predict auspicious times for performing certain actions. These predictions typically include both a day and an hour. Pay attention to astrologers, for their knowledge of dates can also provide us with untapped power. For example, knowing the date and hour of our subject's birth makes it easier for our spells to affect them.

In general, magic becomes more powerful on the first and fifteenth day of the month. Four in the morning and dusk are auspicious times. However, chi drops to its lowest point at three in the morning. This is a time of death.

Numbers also have important significance. 1 is seen as a lonely number, and therefore unlucky. 2 represents ease. 3 signifies living or giving birth. 4 is a dead number. 5 signifies bad luck when combined with certain words. 6 represents longevity. 7 is another dead number. 8 indicates prosperity, and 9 represents mystical influences. When combined these numbers take on additional meanings. For example, 108 is a spiritual number of great significance. Many temples have 108 different fortune sticks in their mixture.

Written Magic

Writing is a type of magic in itself. The written word does not merely represent something. It actually connects to the object it describes. For this reason, writing carries great power. We can accomplish nearly anything through written spells — controlling spirits, taming gods or influencing the weather. They can repel tigers or mosquitoes, drive off bandits, cure headaches or help the dead.

Using stylized calligraphy, mediums and sorcerers write out spells on yellow or black paper. These spells remain inert until activated, by affixing them to the target, placing them under a pillow or burning them. The most common activation for a healing spell involves burning it and mixing its ashes with pure water. The person to be healed then drinks the combination. Notice that the person activating the spell is not necessarily the sorcerer who wrote it.

Written spells and charms are used by both the common people and true sorcerers. Common spells usually involve small healing or protective charms. Most people feel that they can only use magic to help others. Obviously, most true sorcerers disagree, and our knowledge of magic imbibes our written spells with real power.

Written Magic in the Game

Written spells do not last long in areas with a negative Sorcery AV modifier. You must use them within five minutes, or they become simple pieces of paper.

Anyone can activate a written spell. Its potency depends on the sorcerer who wrote it — not the person activating it.

Little People Hitters

The Little People Hitters represent another type of commonplace magic. Typically practiced by old women who dress in black and live on the outskirts of town, these are minor spells cast to punish the cruel, greedy and hurtful (the little people). To hire one such woman, you must bring them the birth date and time of your target. Then, if the target truly deserves to be hit, the spirits will ensure a streak of bad luck.

However, there are no guarantees. Many people seem to be immune to the Little Hitter's magic. Some seem to thrive on it.

Hitters in the Game

The Little People Hitters cannot affect anyone with a Chi score above 0. Barring this, anyone falling under their influence gains all the disadvantages of attunement to a negative feng shui site (see p. 188 of the rulebook). This lasts until they redeem themselves to the person who hired the hitter.

Dieters

Food is also a pathway to supernatural power. While a basic, healthy diet will undoubtedly increase a person's energy, mental alertness and physical fitness, many use exotic diets as a road to greater power.

For example, eating the dust of a 1,000-year-old bat will grant you 40,000 years of life. Some people dissolve jade dust in rice wine, then crystallize it into pills. If you eat these for a year, you will not get wet in water or burnt in fire. After seven years you can walk on water, and eventually you gain immortality.

These mystical diets range from the exotic to the mundane. In general, a mundane food source requires constant and often exclusive consumption — usually taking several years before the eater receives any benefits. For example, Si Tso ate only asparagus for five years before he gained the ability to fly. It took another five before his body began to regenerate. On the other hand, one bite of a 1,000-year-old ginseng root will instantly bring your body into perfect health.

While this path offers great power, it also has many drawbacks. If the dieter breaks from their diet, they will lose whatever powers they gained, and they must start again at the beginning. Many choose starvation over the loss of their powers.

Alchemy

Like written spells, alchemy uses physical objects as a focus for magic. Alchemists create potions with magical abilities. To activate

A young man sought out a Taoist wizard, hoping to become his student. The wizard refused, but the man returned every day for a month, each day begging the wizard to change his mind. Finally, the young man asked if he could just learn one small trick — that way he would not return home empty-handed.

The wizard led the young man into his house and sat him beside the fireplace. The wizard reached his hand into the still glowing embers, lifting out a handful. With a smile, he cast them into the air, where they turned into gold coins. The young man's eyes brightened, but the wizard warned him. "Before I teach you this trick, you must prove to me that you will not use it to feed your greed. Use it to entertain others if you must. But promise that you will always change the gold back." The young man promised, and over the next four months, the wizard trained him.

The young man grew old. He practiced his trick dozens of times, but always carefully collected the coins and cast them back into the fire. At first he was happy and prosperous — but times soon changed. Two years of drought drove his farm into poverty. His children turned against him. During his last days, he found himself alone in a rundown house on the edge of town.

Warming his hands by a small fire, the now-old man smiled. It had been sixty years since the wizard taught him his trick. Surely he would not mind an old man using it to buy a few comforts. Reaching into the fire, he found that — for the first time — the ashes burnt his skin.

The pain caused his vision to blur, but when his eyes cleared, he found himself young again. He sat in the wizard's house with a handful of glowing embers scattered in front of the fireplace.

"So, this is the way you keep your promise, eh?" The wizard asked. The young man sucked on his burnt fingers and bowed his head. He knew the wizard would never teach him now.

— Dr. John Haynes, Dragon Observer, Full-Contact Historian and High-Caliber Anthropologist

the spell, they must drink the potion or spread it over the target. However, unlike written spells, alchemy remains a little-known and highly-suspect art.

In their quest for an elixir of immortality, alchemists handle exacting doses of poisonous herbs and metals. Many rob graves to conduct experiments on the dead. Others kidnap people to test their newest concoctions. All alchemists grow a bit strange, driven insane by the fumes of their mixtures.

Well, that is not entirely true. But it does represent the general opinion on alchemy. While many alchemists do fit the above mold, others use their art to help those around them. Their healing potions restore health and vitality to the sick and injured. Their oils strengthen blades, so they will not break in battle. By carefully following their instructions, you can even add a few decades to your life. They are founts of wisdom and masters of healing, herbalism and anatomy. Unfortunately for them, these alchemists remain burdened with the reputation of their power-hungry brethren.

Jade Fox of Heaven, taoist wizard

Attributes: Bod 4, Chi 8, Mnd 7, Ref 6

Skills: Deceit 12, Infiltration 12, Martial Arts 16, Sorcery 18

Sorcery Shticks: Domination (–2 AV), Fertility (–2 AV), Healing (–2 AV), Influence (+2 AV), Weather (–2 AV)

Fu Shticks: The Fox's Retreat, Eyes of the Fox, Laughter of the Fox, Vengeance of the Fox

Base Damage: 6 (hands)

Notes: Most of the time, Jade Fox of Heaven is content to ignore the world. He lives in a small cave. A waterfall decorates his door. Fresh vegetables grow within five minutes' walk, and when he is very hungry, fish jump from the water into his hand.

Occasionally, though, he descends into Hsia-p'ei. Sometimes he looks for a student. Other times, he simply plays tricks on wealthy merchants or corrupt imperial magistrates. However, since the Lotus arrived in town they have become his favorite target for mischief.

On very rare occasions, Jade Fox of Heaven may try to help the PCs out — though his help will undoubtedly seem annoying and indirect. That is his way.

Taoist Wizards

These strange-robed figures are masters of illusion. They only appear when searching for a new student, when they wish to teach someone a lesson, or when they just want to play pranks on the greedy and self-absorbed. Taoist wizards often take the form of drunks, beggars or other disreputable types.

As they approach their target, they create an entire illusionary world. While wrapped in this world, everything happens according to the wizard's wishes. He can test the target with fantastic monsters and earth-shattering disasters — or he can allow them to live an entire lifetime of wealth, happiness, poverty or misfortune. It all depends on the wizard's goals — and it only takes a few minutes of real time.

Presumably Taoist wizards have mastered other types of magic as well. Illusions are just their favorite.

Si Tso

Attributes: Bod 8, Chi 0 (for 4), Mnd 6, Ref 6
Skills: Gun 10, Info/Magic 10, Martial Arts 16
Creature Shticks: Flight, Regeneration (2 wp/seq)
Base Damage: 9 (hands)
Notes: Despite his creature powers, Si Tso is not a supernatural creature. Also, he cannot eat anything but asparagus, or he will lose these abilities.

Fire Thorn Hoi Mao Qian stepped out from his silk-lined carriage. The driver (one of his vassals) handed him Gao's scroll, then saluted and drove away. Mao fingered the silk ribbon that held it closed. He did not need to open it. He knew what it said.

Slow steps took him down a familiar road. This was his village, the village of his childhood. And before him, perched atop the hill, sat his father's home. He enjoyed the walk, reveling in the sunshine and warm air. Pleasant memories wrapped around him. Playing with his brothers in the nearby woods. Fishing along the river. Festivals to the local gods. Smiling, he stepped up to the house, through the door.

Hoi Zi Yun stood just inside. He looked old – old and weak. A scowl crossed his face, and he reached for the sword at his side. Then his eyes grew wide. "Mao?"

"Yes, father."

"You came. I knew you would come. Our village is in terrible trouble – "

"I know." Mao interrupted, holding the scroll toward his father. "I was told to bring this."

With trembling fingers, Zi Yun accepted the scroll. "Then it is over. They plan to destroy us."

"No father. Not destroy you. Not if you pay the taxes. It's not too late. I can take them back with me. The Emperor will forgive you."

Zi's hand clenched around the still-unopened message. "We cannot pay these. The Emperor asks too much."

"I know." Mao turned to leave. "I'm sorry."

"Son," Mao felt his father's hand touching his shoulder. "Put in a good word for us. We're good people. We don't mind working hard. We just need a little something for winter, a little to trade at market."

Mao did not turn around. "I'll do what I can." He walked out of the house, then turned around for one last look.

"So, how did it go?" the demon Two Ox said, materializing at Mao's side.

"About as I expected."

Two Ox smiled, exposing his sharp, ragged teeth. "Then allow me."

"No. I have waited years for this moment." Mao raised his hands, muttering softly under his breath. The electric fire of magic raced through his arms, pouring into the desired pattern. He held it, as the shape grew strong. Then, just as it threatened to slip from his grasp, he released it.

A rain of fire fell from the sky, igniting both house and field. Mao heard shouting from inside. He saw his father run through he front door, sword in hand. But Mao made a twist of the magic, and the sorcerous fire burst around him. The still-burning corpse of his father collapsed in the yard, dead at the hands of the son he'd given to the Lotus.

"Well done, master."

Mao nodded. "Have the others finish the job. Leave nothing standing, not a single rock. Then meet me back at Lo-yang."

The demon smiled again. "As you wish."

CHAPTER 5

The Four Rules

So, impudent child, you have returned. No, you are still a child. You have come far since we first met, but do not let your accomplishments delude you. This is the beginning, not the end. And if you wish to survive, you must continue to listen to your elders. Remember: the strong survive, and the weak perish. You are weak — but you have the potential to grow strong. Very strong indeed, or I would not waste my breath. So listen, child. Listen and learn.

The first rule is simple: trust no one. I know that your family weaned you on filial piety, but that is a lie. Your ancestors wish to suck away your strength. Do not let them. Use them if you can. Sever the relationship if you cannot. As for our or-der, the same advice applies. Those under you will seek to advance at your expense. Those above will fear you — and try to keep you down. No one looks out for your interests. Not even me.

The second rule: it is best to strike first. Better to act than to react. Better to betray than to be betrayed. Do not delude yourself. It will happen. You must choose whether you will be the victim or the victor.

The third rule: you must retain control over every situation. This is difficult, child. You will encounter those stronger, smarter and faster than you. You must establish your domain, and slap down any opposition. When your opponents begin to tower over you, find their weakness and push hard. Attack decisively and knock them down to their foundations.

The fourth rule: you must learn the secrets of subtlety. This is the hardest to express, but it is the most influential ability you can master. It encompasses everything you do — but appears to be nothing at all. Proper subtlety will win any battle, no matter what the odds. Never reveal the true depths of your goals, knowledge or abilities. Feed from the strong, exploit the weak. Steal the credit for the efforts of others, yet lead blame and trouble to another's doorstep. Most importantly, turn your enemies against one another. In this way, you can destroy without investment.

These are the secrets of our order. Not the sorcery. Not the allies from below. These — and these alone — will lift us above the weak, sniveling factions that oppose us.

Learn them, child. Learn them well. Now, your life begins.

Playing the Lotus

The Eaters of the Lotus can be more than simple villains for the players to pound on (or be pounded on by). If you wish to experiment with unusual campaigns, you could start the characters off as Lotus members. This will allow a lot of room for roleplaying, moral dilemmas, and righteous rebellion. The following sections should help both the GMs and players set up and run a Lotus campaign.

Lotus Campaigns

There are two basic types of Lotus Campaigns: enlightenment and justified. In an enlightenment campaign, the players will eventually learn that they have backed the wrong side. Slowly, they discover the excesses and wrongful manipulations behind the Lotus's glorious claims. Eventually their superiors ask them to take immoral action — or they will find that they have seriously wronged someone while pursuing the Lotus's goals. Once they see the true horror lurking behind the Lotus's façade, they rebel and begin fighting the good fight. These characters almost inevitably join the Dragons, though they might end up with the Hand.

When running an enlightenment campaign, slowly introduce the horrific side of the Lotus. Start with a rumor or two. Then a hint that something might not be right. With each session, continue to up the ante. You probably want to mix this with reasons to stay — offers of power being high on the list, or opportunities to satisfy a melodramatic hook. But keep pushing, until you drive the characters from their masters.

In the justified campaign, the characters remain loyal to the Lotus, even after discovering their true nature. Something justifies this nature. Perhaps the characters believe in the coming Golden Age. They have seen the future and want to change it. Perhaps they simply hate someone else more. No matter what the Lotus do, the characters believe that they are a better choice than the opposition.

In these games, downplay the bad side of the Lotus, while emphasizing the good things that they do (they are doing some good, right?). Focus on the "evil" committed by opposing factions or local groups. Make the characters feel that they are making a difference in the world around them. Also, generously hand out honors and power. Feel free to create a few moral dilemmas and similar problems — but make the Lotus's methods seem justified, at least in the characters' eyes.

In rare cases, you may have a mixed campaign. This happens when some party members rebel, but others remain loyal. While the resulting roleplaying can be interesting for a session or so, prolonged inter-party conflict could eventually destroy the group. Best to have the players pick one side or the other — then retire any characters on the "wrong" side. These characters then become GMCs, and could even be the party's greatest opponents.

Top Ten Reasons to Join the Lotus

10 You want to hang with demonic babes.
9 Evil laughter reduces stress.
8 You won't go blind.
7 You never have to worry about your voice changing.
6 Free access to the Empress's Quarters.
5 Reduces risk of sexually-transmitted diseases.
4 Megalomania is a lifestyle choice.
3 Your current friends refuse to cower properly.
2 You like to toady.
1 You weren't using it anyway.

Why Join the Lotus?

There are four basic reasons to join the Lotus: power, expansion, defense and personal enemies.

Power

Perhaps you flocked to the Lotus's side, seeking power. For some, it is simply better to break knees than to have your own broken. You know which way the wind blows, and have placed yourself upwind of the stink. Others — particularly sorcerous or supernatural characters — will seek out the Lotus, hoping to gain some of the power they control.

Expansion

You see the glory of the Han dynasty and wish to spread it across the globe. A quick look around tells you that simple barbarians occupy all lands beyond the Empire's borders. Still, foreign merchants have brought many tastes of the outside world, and though you hate to admit it, there are a few goods that only come from these barbarians. Surely, the Empire will only grow more glorious once you civilize these lands.

On the other hand, you could have seen the future — or at least heard about it. You know that the Han dynasty is the greatest age since the Sage Emperors. The future will only bring decline, decadence and foreign occupation. You want to strengthen the Empire against the future. You hope that by expanding in both this time and the future you can build a true Golden Age — an age of greatness that will last ten thousand generations.

Defense

You simply wish to protect the Empire from those threatening it. Local threats are ample: barbarian raiders in the north, bandits lurking in the wilderness, rebellious provinces turning away from imperial rule. If left unchecked, these forces will eventually topple the Empire.

Personal Enemies

You just hate someone else more. This typically focuses on one of the other factions. You might be a supernatural creature once captured by the Architects, or a sorcerer trying to keep magic from fading. Perhaps the Jammers blew up large sections of your home town — or you grew up living under the Hand's stifling regime. In any case, working for the Lotus lets you kick their butts on a regular basis. That is good enough for you.

Where in the Lotus

When designing your campaign, you need to decide how the players will fit into the Lotus' organization. Admittedly, few will probably opt to play eunuch sorcerers. Still, they could either become part of the Lotus, or work for one of the many private armies under Lotus control. In the latter case, they probably know nothing about their boss's true connections. They receive orders and report directly to him. He could be a mysterious stranger, a provincial magistrate or a wealthy merchant. The characters may work for the good of the empire, or simply to line their own pockets.

Those working inside the Lotus should start as thorns, either in the Fire or Wood division — these offer the most flexibility, action and independence. However, for a really unusual campaign, the characters could form a team within either the Pillars of Heaven or the Silent Eyes.

Sticking it to them:

Now that your characters work for the Lotus, you should try to make their life uncomfortable. The following suggestions should help you force them to re-evaluate their career choice.

- A greedy Lotus underling decides to manipulate the party, using them to seize power.
- The party must work with demons. If that's not bad enough, the demons begin demanding obedience or sacrifices.
- The party's superior commands them to attack an innocent village. Worse yet, after attacking a "rebel encampment" they discover it was an innocent village.
- They face off against the Dragons. During the second or third skirmish, one of the Dragon warriors accuses the characters of committing heinous crimes (preferably ones that they unknowingly committed, perhaps by summoning monsters and turning them loose). The characters eventually learn that the Dragons are protecting an innocent village — a village the characters plan to attack.
- Their superiors decide to sacrifice the party as a scapegoat.
- Their superiors try to sacrifice one of the characters to their pet demon.
- Two words: suicide mission.

Exploding Brains

For the most part, the Lotus do not trust their underlings. They use a variety of spells to ensure their underlings' prolonged obedience — a particular favorite is the exploding brain. By combining a Blast (fire) and Divination (warning), they can cause severe neural trauma to any underlings who try to betray them.

PC underlings may also have this or similar magicks placed upon them. In these cases, it is important to define exactly what the spell does and how it is triggered. This gives the character an added complication — if they want to turn against their masters, they need to find a way to circumvent the spell. Perhaps they exploit loopholes in the trigger or find a friendly sorcerer to undo it.

In some campaigns you may want to ignore this sorcerous control, or delay it. Their masters will only use the spells after they begin to lose control. Once the characters start to display a bit of rebellion, they find themselves bound by a magical leash.

APPENDIX B

Rules

Magical Artifacts

Many magical artifacts can be found throughout the 69 juncture, from legendary items forged during the age of the Sage Emperors to new constructs created by Lotus sorcerers. These items are often surrounded by myths and legends. The following list includes a few examples.

Note: Most of these items are quite rare. Some have extreme powers. Treat them with caution.

Magical Artifacts & Juncture Modifiers

Magical artifacts will not function in junctures that have a Sorcery AV modifier of –2 or worse. In those junctures, the artifact will behave as a normal item of that type with no special powers; items like the Pocket Demon simply cannot be activated. The Living Staff will not be able to draw chi while it is in such a magic-poor juncture, and will go dormant as per the usual rules for the staff until it returns to a juncture with stronger magic. New artifacts of the GM's devising should follow similar guidelines.

Amulet of the Turtle

This is a plain wooden amulet; however, when worn by someone with the Sorcery skill, it comes to life. The amulet absorbs any damage inflicted on its bearer. It can absorb a number of Wound Points equal to the bearer's Sorcery AV. Any further Wound Points will destroy the amulet (reducing it to broken bits of wood). However, the amulet will heal 5 of the Wound Points it has absorbed each dawn.

Bow of the Tiger Hunt

The Hsiung-nu revere this weapon, first carried by Baun, head of the Cunaan clan. Legends claim that a mysterious stranger gave the bow to Baun's parents, instructing them to hold it until the youth's first hunt. As it happened, that corresponded to the retirement of Gural, the clan's chief.

Gural was old, and had difficulty riding. He wanted to see the Cunaan warriors thundering across the grasslands again, fighting fiercely with their enemies, but he could no longer lead them. Instead, Gural offered his seat to whomever could kill a tiger on the next hunt.

For five days the hunting party rode. They caught many quail and deer, but no one saw a tiger. Then, midway through the sixth day, a cry arose from the far end of the line. One of the hunters spotted, but instead of running, this beast turned and attacked.

Baun watched as it cut a path through the hunters, bringing older warriors down with a single rake of its massive paws. A dozen arrows stuck from its back, but it did not slow. With a snarl, it turned and bolted toward Baun. As those around him fled, the young hunter stood his ground. He nocked an arrow, drew back and let it fly. Before it hit the target, Baun released a second, then a third. The

first arrow sunk deep into the Tiger's neck. The second hit next to it, and the third dove into the beast's shoulder. With a blood-filled roar, the beast launched itself at Baun, landing dead at the boy's feet.

Baun returned to the Cunaan's summer camp, carrying the tiger across his saddle. For twenty-five years he led the Cunaan to glory.

Carved ivory with inlayed gold, the Bow of the Tiger Hunt can be fired easily from horseback or on foot. When using the Bow, each attack costs only 2 shots instead of 3 (this can be further reduced with the Guns schtick Lightning Reload, of course). The wielder also gains +1 to her AV when attacking, +2 if the target is an animal (or transformed animal).

Flying Guillotine

The Flying Guillotine is a one-meter diameter metal ring with sphinctering blades that spiral inwards. Created by the Metal division as a front-line Lotus intimidation weapon, the Flying Guillotine continues to make swooping attacks when thrown until it drops over the target's neck, snipping off the head. Some Flying Guillotines come with mesh bags to hold the severed heads — though most Lotus are not that dramatic. All Flying Guillotines issue a high-pitched howling whistle as they fly.

The Guillotine takes 3 shots to throw, and 1 shot to reset after a successful attack. It has a Ref of 2. It attacks every 3 shots with an AV of 8 and a damage of 15. If the attack kills the target, then it slices off his head. The Guillotine becomes inert until reset and thrown again. If the current target dies before the Guillotine hits, it will pick a random enemy target. For defense purposes, treat the Guillotine as an unnamed character with a defensive AV of 10. If someone "kills" it, it drops to the ground. The Guillotine stays inert until reset and rethrown.

Most Flying Guillotines are keyed to a specific user. That user is the only one who can reset it. Anyone with the Sorcery skill can try to re-key the Guillotine. The attempt takes one hour and has a difficulty of 10.

Jade Armor

This suit of armor consists of intricately-carved jade plates, originally designed as burial armor for the founder of the Tse household in the heavens. However, the Tse ancestors blessed it and returned it to this world — a tool to protect their descendants.

The armor reappeared when bandits threatened Tse Tsing Jinluan's home, suddenly materializing beside his fireplace. Donning the armor and grabbing his sword, Tsing defended his house and family, single-handedly driving back a dozen raiders. Since that time it has passed among both members and servants of the Tse family. No one knows if it will work for someone not aligned to the house.

Note that future historians know that the Tse house will play an important role in the eventual destruction of the eunuchs. Therefore, the Lotus are especially interested in this armor, and would greatly reward anyone who gives it to them.

The armor itself feels uncomfortably stiff and heavy, but when donned, it flows like water around the body. It provides + 4 to the wearer's Toughness, while only subtracting 1 from their Agility. The wearer also does not need food, drink or sleep, and they are immune to sickness and disease. They do not suffer from impairment and regenerate 1 point at the beginning of each sequence.

Unfortunately, long-term exposure to the armor becomes dangerous. Once someone wears the armor for more than two days straight, he will refuse to take it off (Will roll vs. Difficulty 10 to voluntarily remove it; this increases by +1 for each additional day). He becomes a supernatural creature and begins to manifest other Creature Powers — but also becomes cold, calculating and single-minded. He thinks of nothing except the defense of the Tse household. Previous ties with friends or personal goals no longer matter. After a month, he becomes a ghostly warder. The armor then returns to the household.

This transformation is irreversible. First, the character gains Damage Immunity (normal bullets) and Creature Power +1. Then, each week he gains another Schtick, starting with Damage Immunity (hand weapons), and progressing through Insubstantial, Flight and finally Armor (the +6 all at once). With the Armor schtick, the transformation is complete.

The only way to stop the transformation is to pry the armor off the character, and never let him see it again. As long as he can see the Jade Armor, he will do anything to get it back.

Over the centuries, five people have been turned into ghostly warders. They continue to watch the Tse household.

Ghostly Warder

Attributes: Bod 8, Chi 0 (For 3), Mnd 5 (Cha 8), Ref 7

Skills: Creature Power 15, Martial Arts 13

Creature Schticks: Flight, Insubstantial, Damage Immunity: normal bullets and hand weapons, Armor (+6 Tgh)

Jade Javelin

This spear consists of a carved jade tip attached to a sturdy wooden shaft. Carved jade rings are set periodically along the staff. Most of the time the Jade Javelin acts as a normal spear, inflicting Str +4 damage. Once the owner invokes the javelin's power, however, he can throw the javelin with +10 to his AV. Each owner can invoke the javelin's power once. Furthermore, once he invokes the javelin's power it no longer responds properly in his hand. All further attacks have a –2 modifier to his AV.

The owner of the Jade Javelin can pass ownership by simply giving it away willingly. Stealing it or removing it from a dead body does not pass ownership. In that case, a new link must be forged; this requires a sorcery check with a Difficulty of 10.

The Jade Javelin cannot be broken by normal means. Legend says that it will only shatter under the heel of an imperial dragon.

Living Staff

Created by the alchemist Chin Dauning, this staff appears to be simple wood. However, when activated it begins to writhe and grow in the wielder's hands. It takes on a life of its own and can act almost independently of the wielder.

In order to activate the staff, the wielder must feed it 4 Chi points per sequence (this has no shot cost, but the points must be deducted at the beginning of the wielder's first shot of the sequence). This allows the staff to make an additional attack at the same time that the wielder is attacking, with both attacks affecting the same target; the staff has a Martial Arts AV of 14.

During sequences in which the staff has been fed Chi, its damage is the user's Strength +4 as it sends sharpened tendrils burrowing into the target — or simply grows six-inch spines along the striking area.

However, the Living Staff must feed on a continuous supply of chi in order to survive. Each morning, the staff will drain 1 point from someone's Chi score. This drain is temporary, returning after a full 8 hours of sleep — and it does not need to come from the staff's wielder. If the staff does not feed, it becomes dormant. After five days without chi, it will die. Additionally, the staff cannot enter areas with a negative Sorcery AV modifier. Doing so instantly destroys it.

Most people who have seen the staff claim that it is intelligent. On occasions, it seems to warn its master of danger by vibrating slightly. Rarer still, it can self-activate (grabbing the chi it needed from the unsuspecting wielder, causing 5 Wound Points). This is usually a desperate attempt to save its master; however, it once drained enough Chi to kill the current master. Perhaps it found someone that it liked better.

No one knows how intelligent the staff may be, or what goals it might have. Perhaps it secretly controls its wielders — or perhaps it is just a puppy, eager to please.

The Pocket Demon

The pocket demon is a portable supernatural creature — folded like a piece of paper for easy transportation. At its smallest, the pocket demon fits inside a wallet, pocket or belt pouch. While folded, the pocket demon cannot perform any actions. It looks like an ordinary piece of red paper. However, it will obey the commands of anyone who unfolds it, returning to its folded state once finished with its task.

The Pocket Demon must sleep in its folded state for at least eight hours a day — otherwise it will automatically fold itself. It takes three shots to unfold the demon.

Sword of the Dragon King

The Dragon King Anchen Hanoun forged this sword from his own scales and blood. He spent ten years crafting the green metal blade, reworking it until its surface shimmered like moonlight off a still pond.

When the Dragon King's daughter fell in love with the human Chuang Ko, Anchen agreed to marry the two. His sword became part of his daughter's dowry, his guarantee that the son-in-law would rise above other mortals.

For twenty years, Chuang Ko carried the sword, earning honor for himself and his father-in-law. He cleared all manner of monsters from the land around Anchen's lake. He fought in a dozen great battles, both creating and destroying kingdoms. Finally, after a life of heroism, Chuang died and Anchen reclaimed the blade.

Anchen knew that other heroes would wield the sword — but he did not want them to overshadow his son-in-law's legend. He carried the blade far into the mountains, burying it at the bottom of a deep cave.

Here the legend grows vague. Some stories claim that 500 years later, new heroes uncovered the blade and carry it still. Others believe that it still lies buried deep beneath the ground.

The Sword of the Dragon King grants its wielder the ability to breathe and move freely underwater. He can swim as quickly as he can run and can even walk on the water's surface, providing it remains sufficiently still. Furthermore, he will emerge from the water perfectly dry — not a drop on himself, his clothes or the gear he carries.

The sword can also summon rain. This requires the wielder to make a fortune roll, with the difficulty based on his climate and region. In humid areas or during rainy seasons, the difficulty is 2. In a desert or during a drought, the difficulty rises to 10. The wielder can also attempt to create floods. This requires a similar fortune roll, with a difficulty of 10 for a flood plain when the river is already high. A difficulty of 20 allows him to create floods in the middle of a desert, with no source of water in sight. This results in minor flooding, damaging simple buildings and temporarily washing out roads. If the wielder wants more-extensive flooding, increase the difficulty by 3 or 5 points.

Finally, when used in combat, the sword increases the wielder's Martial Arts AV by +1, +2 if used underwater. Damage is normal: Strength + 4.

NEW RULES FOR MAGIC

This section includes a wide variety of useful things. Various ways to augment or modify spells are covered, as are new forms of magic such as alchemy and artifact creation. New spells, new special effects for existing spells, and new supernatural creature abilities round out the selection.

Ritual Magic

The basic rules for magic handle most situations, most of the time. But occasionally you will try to stretch the bounds of your power. Through careful study, planning and organization, you can reach powers otherwise unavailable. The following guidelines will help you create more-powerful spells by granting you additional magic points, letting you use assistants, and use sacrifices.

Research

Research is the first step in any ritual. You must spend at least one hour going through scrolls, books, speaking with spirits, meditating or any other appropriate action to get additional magic points for your spell. After this, make a Sorcery skill check. The difficulty depends on the maximum number of magic points you wish to generate. You must spend these points while casting the spell, or they are lost.

Research

Difficulty	Maximum Magic Points
5	1
7	2
10	3
15	5
20	10
25	15
30	30

After determining the maximum magic points, the GM then decides what the sorcerer must do to earn them. This may include lengthy casting times, unusual spell components, or any number of other time-consuming or hard-to-find things. The GM does not need to allocate a full slate of points — though he should try to give out at least half the max. The more requirements that the PCs meet, the more points they should get.

Note: If the resulting ritual is unacceptable to the sorcerer, he can always try again. However, any additional research adds a cumulative +5 modifier to the difficulty each time it is attempted.

Research is only good for one attempt at casting the spell. Future attempts require additional research. The GM may also place limits on how long you can wait before casting the spell.

GM Note: If a player attempts to use a ritual to create something that derails the plot, is overly subtle, is boring or just plain cheesy you should either rule the efforts to be an automatic failure or set ridiculous conditions to be met in order to perform the ritual. If a player is attempting to use a ritual for something that enables him to bypass certain obstacles in the scenario, make sure that the conditions they have to meet in the ritual pose equally difficult and entertaining challenges.

Multicasters

Additional Magicians	Magic Points
1	1
10	2
20	3
30	4
(each ten additional assistants above 30 grant an additional point)	

Additional Help

You can use a group of fellow sorcerers to produce a more powerful effect by making additional Magic points to use in casting the spell. Everyone in the group must have the appropriate schtick — though not necessarily the appropriate special effect. Choose someone to act as the leader. Use his abilities to make all rolls, gaining the additional points listed in the table above.

Note: Besides the points given in the chart, both the lead sorcerer and the assistants can add their magic points to the spell. The leader's magic points add as normal. Assistants must spend 10 points (collectively) to add a single point. So if four assistants each put in three points (for a total of 12), the leader gets one additional magic point to use in the spell; round points added to the nearest 10.

Sacrifice

For those truly on the fast track to power, you can boost your spells with the traditional human sacrifice. You gain a number of magic points equal to the victim's Magic statistic + 1, which can only be used for purposes of the ritual spell. If not used for that purpose, they are lost.

You are free to sacrifice anyone. Optionally, the GM can require you to sacrifice a particular person. This will give an additional +1 to +4.

Remember: This sacrifice requires ritual murder. Killing someone during combat does not count. Also, the person must die, and must stay dead. Needless to say, heroic PCs shouldn't be conducting human sacrifices (barring outrageous circumstances or a truly nasty streak), but GMC villains are likely to.

Non-Ritual Bonuses

You can always opt to use the following to generate additional magic points. As with ritual magic, you must use these points while casting the spell. Of course, the GM could also require these elements as part of a ritual.

Auspicious Time

With a successful Divination check, you can predict an appropriately auspicious time for the spell in question. The difficulty depends on how soon you want the time to be. If the difficulty is 30, it will fall sometime within the next 24 hours. If the difficulty is 10, it will happen any time in the next six months. Auspicious times always include both a date and an hour.

If the outcome is 0–4, you gain a magic point when you cast the spell at the prescribed time. On 5 or more, gain two. On 10 or more, gain three — and so on.

Note: The person divining the auspicious time does not have to be the same one casting the spell; the points are gained when the spell is cast at the right moment, not when the right moment is divined.

If the GM establishes an auspicious time for a ritual and the research for the ritual includes figuring out that time through means other than Divination, no rolls are required. The GM simply sets an appropriate magic point bonus.

Power Over Target

Knowing someone's name, birth date and birth hour enhances any spell cast on them. You can either gain one Magic Point for purposes of that spell only, or you can cast a spell on your target even when the target is outside your line of sight. For these indirect spells, add +10 to the difficulty. The target must be within 10 km.

Spell Enhancements

The following list includes various methods for enhancing or otherwise beefing up a spell. Though they are all technically stunts, each has a unique cost or requirement.

Alchemy and Written Magic

Any sorcerer can create written spells and potions. This counts as a stunt with a -2 AV modifier. For more information, see the earlier descriptions of Alchemy and Written Magic. Also, look at the Alchemist unique schtick in the types section.

Area of Effect

You can give a spell an area of effect by spending 1 magic point per 1m radius. The spell will then affect all appropriate targets within that area — friends and enemy alike.

Binding Supernatural Creatures

While the Summoning (Domination) effect allows you to issue commands to supernatural creatures, it does not provide long-term control. For the Lotus, this was unacceptable. They rely on a host of demons, monsters and spirits to control the land and crush their opponents. They needed to rely on their supernatural minions' loyalty day after day, month after month, year after year. Some sorcerers bind their summoned creatures into physical objects — only releasing them when necessary. Unfortunately, this only delays the inevitable. It does not extend the actual duration of control.

Ritual Magic in the Game

Ritual magic is primarily intended for GM characters. Their elaborate requirements for nefarious magic can easily form the background for a plot, with a ritual site making a potentially exciting battlefield. Player characters should focus on action, not long, complicated procedures. They should try to save people from the sacrificial dagger — not cut them open.

Still, there are times when ritual magic may be thematically appropriate. Note that this should almost always occurs during down time. It falls into the same category as training or healing. In these cases the GM should create generously easy (yet still appropriate) rituals.

In other cases, the characters might need a ritual to prevent a disaster. Here, the plot line revolves around fulfilling whatever requirements the GM sets (e.g., gathering the appropriate props before the auspicious time passes).

However, the GM should deal harshly with anyone who tries to use ritual magic instead of action. Anyone bogging down the plot deserves what they get.

There are basically two ways to ensure long-term control over a supernatural creature. The first is to cast a permanent Domination spell. Unfortunately, this typically involves a long ritual including a human sacrifice and a dozen sorcerers working together. Still, this remains the favorite route of high-power Petals.

The second way is more dangerous, but open to anyone. Here, you simply negotiate with the supernatural creature. Most demons will readily agree to service, starting at a surprisingly-insignificant cost. But don't act surprised when they renegotiate their contract — usually during a fight scene. Other creatures have their own morals and ticket prices.

Once the negotiations are complete, most sorcerers ensure continuing loyalty with a warded blast spell. If the supernatural creature tries to harm or betray them, the spell goes off. Of course, an enterprising sorcerers may attempt to trap a supernatural creature into servitude by just casting the warded blast spell on him. However, this only works on the weakest of creatures. Any demon worth his spines can shrug off a fire blast or two — though the sorcerer may not fare as well once the demon gets its hands on him.

Permanent Magic

Most magic spells are fleeting, but that's generally all you need. In its split-second existence, the lightning bolt burns a hole in the chest of an opposing swordsman, and your fly spell lasts long enough to escape from a 20-story window — hopefully. However, there are times you may want to leave a permanent mark on the world.

Unless the schtick or special effect says otherwise, you can make any spell permanent by spending 20 magic points while casting it.

Note: this only works in an area with a positive Sorcery AV modifier.

Remember, the spell is permanent — not necessarily its effect. A permanent Fire Blast may create a constantly burning ball of fire, but the damage it causes will heal normally. You could use it to create an interesting monument, or as a power source — but its attack value remains relatively unchanged (provided your opponent has the common sense to move after taking the initial hit). In many cases, the GM must decide the exact effect of spell permanence.

While permanent magic can be a great boon, it can also turn dangerous. Long-term exposure to magical energies has a tendency to create physical and mental changes in the target. A magically-augmented character might slowly slip into madness, or develop a debilitating disease. Reactions include psychotic behavior, exotic allergies, constant headaches, poor healing, personality changes and so forth. Even inanimate objects have a tendency to change slowly after time — often gaining characteristics symbolic of the magic at work.

NEW SORCERY SCHTICKS

Here are a few new schticks to round out your sorcerer's abilities.

Animalism

This schtick involves highly-shamanistic abilities, all focused on animals.

Influence Animals: Difficulty of 12. You can add your outcome to any charisma-based skills while interacting with animals. **Note:** this works on transformed animals, but once they realize you are using magic, their anger is likely to outstrip any benefits you gained.

Speak With Animals: Difficulty 10. This allows you to speak to animals — including transformed animals who speak foreign languages. It does not, however, guarantee that the animal has anything worthwhile to say. To most animals, all humans look alike — and all human activity is universally inexplicable. Still, this dialogue can last for a number of minutes equal to your outcome.

Summon Animals: Difficulty 15. As soon as you cast this effect, animals of a chosen sort will begin to arrive — one the next sequence, with an additional one every sequence thereafter. You gain a total number of animals equal to your outcome. Of course, this only works if the appropriate animals live in the area (within 1 km or so). **Note:** These animals arrive under their own power — they are not magically

transported. Also, this effect does not guarantee that they will be friendly. (Yes, you can summon transformed animals. They usually arrive carrying big guns.)

Create Magical Artifact

As the name implies, you use this schtick to create new magical items. Backlash indicates that the object in question is somehow ruined.

Note: this schtick may encourage sorcerous PCs to waste valuable game time pumping up their allies. This is the kiss of death to action storylines. To prevent this, the GM may require rituals to use this schtick — or may restrict it to GMCs only.

However, if used properly this schtick can add an interesting flavor to the game. Priestly sorcerers may distribute good luck charms to any they meet. Also, the creation of a powerful artifact is an appropriate long-term goal.

Enhancement: This special effect enhances the abilities of an object. An enhanced sword will have an improved balance with an unusually-sharp edge, while an enhanced serving bowl will improve the quality of any food it contains. The exact result varies.

Note: The following examples are for enhanced weapons. The GM must choose similar effects for non-weapon enhancements.

The enhancement lasts for a number of sequences equal to the outcome. One magic point extends this to hours, a second to days.

Artifact Creation

Difficulty	Effect
20	Acts as a Signature Weapon for the bearer. If cast on someone's signature weapon, this has no effect.
25	+1 AV
30	+2 AV

Good Luck: Difficulty 17. This imbues the object with a single Fortune die. This die remains until used, and can be tapped by anyone holding the object. Typically, each object can only have one Good Luck cast upon it. Additional Good Luck castings on the same object raise the difficulty by 4 (21 for the second, 25 for the third, and so on).

Grant Creature Ability: You can lend an object the abilities of a supernatural creature that has been Object Bound into it (see Summoning [Object Bind] on p. 99). If the creature is willing, Grant Creature Ability has a difficulty of 5. However, the granted powers remain under the creature's control. He decides when to trigger it, and who it targets.

For unwilling creatures, the difficulty equals the supernatural creature's Will. The outcome determines the number of powers that you gain access to. In either case, you must decide whether the power will affect the object or the object's wielder (as if the wielder possesses the creature ability). Grant Creature Ability lasts until the supernatural creature is released.

Repeat Spell: Difficulty 20. The object will absorb the next spell cast into it, and can then repeat the spell a number of times equal to the Repeat Spell outcome. The object must absorb the new spell within 2 sequences of casting Repeat Spell. You can even use Repeat Spell defensively, to absorb incoming spells; however, this requires you to parry the spell with the object. Your defensive AV is reduced to your Martial Arts –2.

When the object recasts the repeated spell, reroll the outcome as a newly-cast spell using the original caster's AV (but no bonuses for magic points spent). You do not need to be a sorcerer to release the held spells — you simply need to know the trigger, set at the time of casting. Triggers can include movements or code phrases, but are usually a combination of the two. Releasing a spell costs 3 shots. Spells stored in an object will remain there indefinitely, but if the object is taken into a juncture with a –2 Sorcery AV modifier or worse, all stored spells are lost.

Transmutation

While the Blast (Transmutation) effect changes objects and people to cause damage, the Transmutation schtick allows you to alter objects for productive reasons. Backlash indicates that the transmutation goes out of control. This can result in the target being trapped in an unwanted form (for as long as the GM considers it dramatically appealing), or it could cause 10 Wound Points in transmutation damage. All changes last one hour per point of outcome — or one day if you spend a magic point.

Warning: Prolonged or continual transmutations can have harmful effects. If you wear a different shape for more than one day, you must make a Willpower check (base difficulty 5, and +2 every day you are transmuted), or you lose your identity and become the new shape permanently. Also, continual transmutations will eventually weaken your body's shape-identity. You may find that your body begins shifting on its own. Sometimes it will lose cohesion and ooze into a gray puddle. At other times, it will begin sprouting odd physical features. On occasion, you may feel sharp internal pains for no apparent reason.

The cure for both problems is the same. Go to an area with a negative Sorcery AV, and stay there for a while. A week or a month should do. If the symptoms persist, see a sorcerous doctor.

Augment Form: This lets you enhance the target. Each point of outcome can increase a secondary attribute by one point (maximum of 4 each). Similar bonuses can be allowed in inanimate objects at the GM's discretion. Living creatures have a difficulty of 17. Inanimate objects have a difficulty of 15.

Matter Shift: This lets you change the type of matter: lead to gold, flesh to stone, and so forth. Again, difficulties vary depending on the degree of change but should begin at 15 for simple shifts.

Partial Shifts: Similar to shape shift, but instead of changing the whole form, it only changes parts. For example, you could give the target gills, an armored hide, or tiger claws. Difficulty of 15.

Shape Shift: This allows you to change one object to another. The difficulty depends on the degree of change between the various forms. Changing someone's sex is relatively simple (Difficulty 10), while turning a pile of silicon into a computer would be incredibly difficult (Difficulty 25). Generally, this will not let you change the type of matter — just its current form. A person to plant change is possible. Person to stone is not. However, the target gains all natural benefits and limitations of the new form. This does not include Creature Abilities, Fu Powers and similar supernatural stuff.

NEW SPECIAL EFFECTS

Here are new special effects to go with your new schticks.

Blast

Bolt of Force: Kinda like taking a sledgehammer to the stomach. This invisible punch is great for knocking people over, breaking down doors, or setting off the airbags during a car-chase scene.

Earthquake Wave: By striking the ground with a staff, stomping, or some similar maneuver, you create a wave of tremors moving toward the target. The Earthquake Wave damages buildings, walls, automobiles and other large objects. Target characters must make a Martial Arts check (difficulty equals the sorcery Action Result) to remain standing. Though they take no damage from the wave, its ancillary effects might harm them.

Debris could fall on them, or the sidewalk could collapse from underneath.

The basic wave is 1m wide, and moves in a straight line. For 1 magic point, you can create a wave that spreads into a cone of destruction. For 2 magic points, it forms an expanding circle around the caster. The caster is not affected by the wave, but could be hurt by a nearby falling building or other ancillary effect.

The wave does normal blast damage to buildings and other structures. Most of the time this does little more than shatter glass and weaken the structure. Actually collapsing a building would require a stunt.

Flaming Ash: This creates a stream of hot coals and burning ash. Basically a primitive napalm, this tends to stick to the target and cause continuing pain. If your target loses more than 10 Wound Points, the ash will cause 1 point of impairment until scraped off. It ignites anything flammable. Also used to create a pre-lit barbecue.

Light: A high intensity flash. Causes no damage, but the target is blinded for a number of shots equal to the outcome. For 1 magic point, everyone looking at the caster is affected.

Magical Disruption: While this blast will harm supernatural creatures (it disrupts their chi flow), it is primarily designed for destroying spells and disabling magical artifacts. For spells, the difficulty equals the original caster's sorcery AV. If successful, the spell is destroyed. Items have a difficulty of 10. They are disabled for a number of sequences equal to the outcome. When used against a supernatural creature, it does normal Blast damage.

Object Overload: While the Lotus initially had trouble with technology, they quickly learned to use it to their advantage. This effect causes a small technological item to malfunction, damaging the wielder. Perhaps the ammo explodes in the target's gun, or his computer short circuits, arcing electricity at the user. Regardless, the base damage is equal to half your Magic, and then +1 on top of that — but it almost always destroys the object in question. Also useful for blacking out phones and cutting off the power to buildings. **Note:** This is useful for taking out hand-held weapons, or one small (and largely unnecessary) aspect of a more complex machine. But don't try to use it to take out a fusion tank! Its communication system, maybe. Also, signature weapons are immune to Object Overload.

Thunder: BOOM! Target is deaf for a number of sequences equal to the outcome. Must make a constitution check against the spell's Action Result or is stunned. Subtract the outcome from their remaining shots, carrying over to the next sequence. Thunder blasts can also shatter windows. Thunder blast attacks are made at –1 AV, but inflict +1 damage.

Water: Creates a firehose stream of water. Puts out fires, quickly cleans automobiles, fills swimming pools. The target must make a Martial Arts check to remain standing (difficulty equals the Sorcery Action Result). Base damage equals the caster's Magic –2. Additional water damage and flooding are possible.

Wind: Good for blowing out fires, parrying volleys of arrows, scattering important documents and turning umbrellas inside out. Wind attacks cause no damage, but knock the target backwards a number of meters equal to the user's outcome. The target must make a Martial Arts check to remain standing (Difficulty equals the Sorcery Action Result –5). Flying targets typically require an appropriate skill check or they lose control (Difficulty equals the Sorcery Action Result + 5). Additional stunts include creating instant sandstorms and capsizing sailboats.

Divination

Borrowed Ears: This works exactly like the eye-borrowing version of Remote Viewing (described later in this schtick), except that it allows you to hear your subject instead of seeing them (or through them).

Medium: This allows you to open yourself up to spirits, ghosts and lurking demons either hidden in this world, the underworld or other afterlife realms. Others can then ask the spirit questions. The spirit speaks through you, either using your voice or another method of divination, like fu kay. During the process you are cut off from your body. You cannot do anything. However, you have a vague sense of your surroundings, and can reclaim control at any time (takes 3 shots and ends the effect). Difficulty is 10 for spirits hidden in this world, 15 for spirits in another. You cannot force a spirit to talk with you, they must be a willing participant. **Note:** On a backlash, your body becomes possessed by a demon or hungry ghost. This usually lasts for a single scene — though some will remain until exorcised.

Remote Viewing: Allows you to see far-off places. This typically involves staring into a reflective pool, crystal ball, mirror, blazing fire or similar focus. You can look in on people, places or things that you know. The difficulty depends on the distance between you and the target.

This effect has two different versions. The first version gives you a remote view of your target, as if you were standing about 10m away. The second lets you look through the target's eyes. Remote Viewing lasts a number of sequences equal to your outcome. Spending 1 Magic point increases that to hours. **Note:** This effect does not let you see in the dark; however, if you borrow someone's eyes you gain any vision advantages or disadvantages they may have.

Divination

Distance	Difficulty
1 km	10
Same City	15
Same Juncture	20
Different Juncture	25

Summoning

Awaken Spirit: Difficulty 10. This allows you to wake the spirit of an inanimate object (see Inanimate Spirits, p. 59). You can also use this to reactivate magical items or supernatural creatures that became dormant due to a negative Sorcery AV Modifier.

Object Bind: This allows you to trap a supernatural creature inside an item. Typical examples include gems, bottles, lamps and such. The creature remains inside the item until it is broken (the sorcerer can create another appropriate trigger — this is just the most common). If combined with Dominate, the creature must then obey the commands of the person releasing them (see Summoning [Dominate]). The base difficulty equals the target's Creature Power AV.

The following creature powers modify the difficulty:

Summoning

Power	Difficulty
Insubstantial	–5
Transformation	–2

Note: While bound into the object, the creature has a limited ability to sense their surroundings. However, they cannot perform any actions (see Grant Creature Ability, p. 96).

Cruel Combinations for Dear Friends

While Sorcery effects can be quite powerful alone, creative combinations allow you to create nearly any effect. The following are a few samples to get your evil juices flowing, using special effects from the main rulebook as well as from this chapter.

Chi Ripper

This combines the Steal Chi and Chi Blast effects. Here you rip Chi from your target's body with enough force to actually injure them. By adding the Harvest Chi effect, you can absorb the stolen Chi into yourself.

Horror Form

An expansion of Living Metal Armor (below). This adds tiger-like claws and protruding razor-sharp blades. The Conjure Weapons effect animates these into a bloodletting blur. Difficulty 20, Armor +5, hand-to-hand damage increases to Strength +5. Lasts for the Outcome in segments, or hours if you spend a magic point.

Living Metal Armor

Partial Shift gives you an insect's exoskeleton. Matter Shift turns it into steel. Augment Form increases your Strength and Agility, to compensate for the added weight and encumbrance. Difficulty 15, Armor +5, no Agility modifier. Lasts for a number of segments equal to the outcome; 1 magic point increases that to Hours.

Rift

Combines Earthquake Wave and Chucking Things About. This creates a hole or chasm; the difficulty depends on the size you want. (See table below.) If you try to cast the spell under someone, their Dodge AV is added is the difficulty (which is still based on how big of a hole you want to make). Anyone falling into the rift takes an appropriate amount of falling damage.

Rift

Difficulty	Size
10	Man-sized hole, 5m deep
15	Man-sized hole, 10m deep or a 10m long, 5m wide, 5m deep chasm.
20	10m x 5m x 10m chasm or a 20m long, 5m wide, 5m deep chasm.
+5	Add +5m to any one of the above dimensions Cannot exceed 10m deep.

They're Everywhere

By combining Illusion and Blast, you can create a horde of unnamed demons who crawl out of the shadows and attack the spell's victim. The difficulty equals the victim's Chi or Magic rating +10. The spell creates a number of demons equal to the outcome. They last until destroyed, or until the target goes unconscious. Any damage they inflict is real. **Note:** only the target sees the demons, and only the target can affect or be affected by them.

Walkie-Talkie

This is a double Borrowed Ears cast on a pair of people. They both hear anything that either could normally hear. Though a little confusing at first, this lets them talk freely, among other things. The difficulty is based on the maximum range (use the table under Remote Viewing). Duration is normal.

Wonderful World of Wards

The basic rules already discuss combining Warning with the Blast schtick. To expand the idea a bit, you can use this combination for nearly any spell, and as a stunt, assign nearly any action as the trigger. **Note:** the more complex the trigger, the more difficult the warning spell will be. Still, you could cast a healing spell on yourself, triggered either when you take damage, when you take more than 5 points of damage from one shot, or when your Wound Points are greater than 20. Each of these is progressively more difficult (15, 20, and 25 respectively). A slightly more-evil combination would involve an area of effect blast spell that goes off once your heart stops beating. This guarantees that you will have the last laugh in any combat, but you'd better hope your sweetheart isn't cradling your corpse as life slips away.

Lotus sorcerers are especially fond of creating wards that will cause their minion's heads to explode should they do anything wrong. These spells are especially powerful because the victims voluntarily accepted them. If an unnamed character sets off his mental bomb, he is dead. Named characters take twice the blast spell's normal damage (ouch!).

Each target can only have one ward active at a time. Old wards must be triggered or dispelled before a new one will take hold. Also, the ward's trigger can only include things that happen to the warded object.

Note: As a stunt, anyone with Blast (Magical Disruption), can try to prematurely trigger the ward. The difficulty should be modified depending on how well they know the ward in question.

Wound Transfer

You transfer damage from one person and inflict it on another, even during combat. Touch the person who need to be healed, and then make a single Blast attack against the target to be injured as per the rulebook; this attack is at –2 AV. The damage inflicted against the target by the Blast spell is also subtracted from the person being healed. If the damage is more than the wounded character's current wound points, only the existing wound points are healed and only that amount of points is dealt to the victim of the Blast. This lets you heal during combat, and attack at the same time.

NEW CREATURE ABILITIES

Just so the supernatural creatures don't feel left out.

Attack Rebound

Each time you are attacked in a specified way, you may attempt to rebound the attack. Your attacker makes her roll, giving you the Action Result (AV + die roll). You then make a Creature Powers check. If it exceeds the Action Result, you can bounce the attack back at its originator. The attack is resolved as if he just attempted to strike himself — using his original rolls. You can also try to bounce an attack towards a new target or perform similar stunts. The modifiers for these are applied to your Creature Power AV. If you fail the check, the attack proceeds normally and you may dodge, etc.

Each schtick spent on Attack Rebound allows you to bounce one specified type of attack — see Damage Immunity in the rulebook for a list of possible attack types.

Blindspot

People do not notice you. This is not invisibility; people who know you can spot you with ease. If someone else looks for you in normal circumstances, they can make a Perception check with your Creature Power AV as the difficulty. If successful, they can see you. Others, however, will simply blot out your existence. They will not walk into you or anything — their subconscious steers them out of your way — but they otherwise ignore you. It is possible that a deep hypnosis could release the suppressed memories of your passage. They would then see you the next time they run into you. A really enterprising guard may locate you by the way others avoid your space — but this is very difficult, since your blind spot makes that seem normal too.

Blindspot will not work if you are making gross physical actions such as firing a gun, running in front of a car, or charging someone.

Blaze of Glory

When you die, your body explodes. This causes 25 points of damage (before Toughness) to anyone within 1m. Anyone else within 10m takes 10 points.

Body Borrow

You have the ability to possess or otherwise control someone's body. You must first touch your target, requiring a Martial Arts check. Then roll your Creature Power against their Will + 10 or their highest AV +2, whichever is higher. You then control their body for a number of sequences equal to the outcome. At that point, repeat the roll — if you succeed, you keep control for a number of hours equal to the outcome. A third successful roll lets you keep the body as long as you wish, or until exorcised.

While in control of the body, you can use it as if it were your own. In general, use the target body's abilities for Body and Reflexes, your own statistics for Chi, Mind and Skills. You also gain access to their Transformed Animal Abilities, Creature Abilities and Arcanowave gear — but you must use your own skills to operate them (If you don't have Arcanowave Device, tough luck). You keep your own Fu Powers, Gun Schticks, Signature Weapons and Magic Schticks. For each additional Schtick you spend, you can port one of your Attributes or Creature Abilities into the borrowed body. Choose the ported ability when you purchase the Schtick.

When adopting the body of a Transformed Animal, it gains +1 Reversion point and must instantly make a Reversion check. If it transforms back, you go with it — becoming forever a dumb animal. As long as you remain inside the Transformed Animal's body, add +1 to the surrounding Sorcery AV when distributing Reversion points.

You must also determine the fate of your own body. If you have either the Insubstantial or Transformation Schtick, you can absorb your body into the target. Otherwise, your body remains catatonic until you return. This is quite dangerous. If your body is destroyed while you are gone, you have one Sequence to possess another body or you die.

If the body you are occupying dies, you are disoriented for a Sequence. You then have one Sequence to find a new body, or you snap back into your own. Snapping back disorients you for another Sequence.

Note: Body Borrow also lets you hitch a ride in someone's body. This only requires one roll. You can then hear anything they hear, see anything they see. But you do not control the body. In fact, they must make a Sorcery check with an action result greater than your AV to detect your presence.

Burning Blood

A spurt of flaming blood automatically attacks anyone who wounds you in close combat. This is a free attack, costing no shots, and occurs immediately. The blood has an AV of 12 and a base damage of 8. Each additional schtick can either increase the AV by +1 or the damage by +2.

Burrowing

You can burrow through the ground at a quarter of your movement. Solid stone and concrete reduce this to an eighth. You cannot burrow through heavy steel walls (like those of a bank vault) or reinforced bunkers. You must decide when taking this schtick whether your burrowing leaves behind usable tunnels. Spending a second schtick allows you to alternate between leaving and not leaving tunnels at will.

Crawling Claws

Your body parts continue to operate, even when detached. If someone chops off your hand, it will continue to attack on its own (using grapple or claw attacks). A removed eye will allow you to see whatever it is pointed at. This does not grant you any special healing or damage immunity; however, if you have two schticks in Crawling Claws, your body parts become removable. You can pop them off and snap them into place without taking any damage — but if someone eats your hand or whatever while it's crawling around, you're out of luck.

Damage Transfer

By touching someone, you can transfer Wound Points between the two of you — you get better, and your target takes damage (or vice versa, if desired). This requires both a Martial Arts and Creature Power check against the target's Dodge AV. You can transfer points equal to your Creature Power Outcome, plus 5 Wound Points per schtick spent on Damage Transfer (e.g., a person with 2 schticks in Damage Transfer will transfer 10 points plus their Creature Power Outcome). This number cannot exceed the number of Wound Points available, however. Using Damage Transfer on a willing target does not require any rolls. Furthermore, you can transfer as many Wound Points as you want.

Envelope Attack

This allows you to wrap around, absorb or otherwise swallow someone whole. Unnamed characters are incapacitated or killed (your choice). Named characters continue to take 5 Wound Points per sequence (this damage is not modified by Toughness or armor). Your victim's ability to continue acting depends on the number of schticks you spent on Envelope Attack, to a maxium of three; see the chart below.

You can hold more than one victim at a time. The number of victims you can hold is equal to the number of schticks you have in Envelope Attack; however, each additional person lowers the impairment shown on the chart by one step. For example, a Demonic Frog with 3 schticks in Envelope Attack could have up to three people trapped — but they could all act normally, since the two additional victims move the impairment down two steps on the chart. Of course, they're still taking damage anyway.

Finally, anyone attacking you risks damaging the victims you have swallowed. Unless an attack made against you has an Outcome of 2 or more, one of your victims takes half the damage. Of course, you still take full damage.

Envelope Attack

Schticks	Enveloping Impairment
1	can act as normal.
2	-2 to all AVs
3	-3 to all AVs, +1 to all shot costs

Voice Mimicry

As you listen to people talk, you can pick up their tone and vocal mannerisms. This requires a Creature Power check, with the difficulty depending on the amount of time you spend studying the target (5 if you've known them for years, 20 if you hear them speak for a minute or less). If this succeeds, you can imitate their voice. At the GM's discretion, another Creature Power check may be required to fool people who know the target well (Difficulty 10 for their coworkers, 15 for their best friends).

Note: You will need to repeat the initial roll if you have not used the voice or encountered the target during a given day; a penalty of +5 to the difficulty is also added for each additional day that passes without encountering the person or using the voice. This represents your attempts to remember it. Once you blow the roll, you cannot use the voice until you listen to the target again.

Will Not Die

No matter how much damage you take, you will not die. However, this does not prevent pain, impairment and unconsciousness. Your ability to handle pain depends on the number of schticks spent on Will Not Die. Unlike normal characters, there is no limit to the number of Impairment points you can gain.

To take this power during character creation, you must spend 2 schticks to get one schtick in Will Not Die; additional schticks in Will Not Die above your first one are purchased normally, however. If you want to gain this power during the course of play by spending experience points, your initial purchase is made at four times the normal cost; again, additional schticks taken to improve your ability with Will Not Die in the future are priced normally once the first schtick has been bought at higher cost.

At 1 schtick, you gain your first point of impairment at 10 Wound Points. You gain an additional point of Impairment every 5 Wound Points thereafter. If your Wound Points ever exceed your Constitution, you must make a Con check (Difficulty = Current Impairment + 10) or fall unconscious.

Each additional schtick you spend delays the initial Impairment point for another 5 Wound Points (15 at 2 Schticks, 30 at 5).: Many undying supernatural creatures are actually more susceptible to minor damage — probably because they tend to stand there and take it.

Finally, you do not automatically heal back to normal between sessions. Whenever the other PCs are allowed to automatically heal, you only regain 10 Wound Points.

NEW UNIQUE SCHTICKS

These unique schticks allow you to customize existing types from the rulebook into types better-suited for the 69 juncture.

OLD MASTER

Retired Soldier: When following one of the Old Master's combat plans, all characters gain +1 Tgh and +1 Damage for the duration of the fight. (This is intended for an Old Master who has military experience with the imperial army.)

To get this schtick during character creation, take it instead of the one given. To add this schtick to your already-existing Old Master, spend 12 experience points.

SORCERER

Alchemist: You focus your magic through potions, powders and similar substances. Each potion takes one hour to make, and they remain inert until activated. This is the only way you can cast spells.

Anyone can activate your potion. The Action Result is determined when you create it by making a Sorcery check as normal.

To use the potion, the user typically drinks it, anoints their body with it, or throws it at a target. You drink Healing, Transmutation, Divination and Influence potions. You anoint the target with a Movement potion. Blast potions and powders are tossed at the target, exploding on impact. All others require similar, appropriate triggers and are up to the GM.

In emergencies, you can quickly mix together raw ingredients to gain an on-the-spot effect. This counts as a desperate effort, costing 1 Magic Point. Furthermore, you can only

count half the Outcome when determining the results.

You can only take this schtick during character creation; it may not be purchased with experience points. To take it, lower your Sorcery AV by one point and take 4 Sorcery schticks instead of 5.

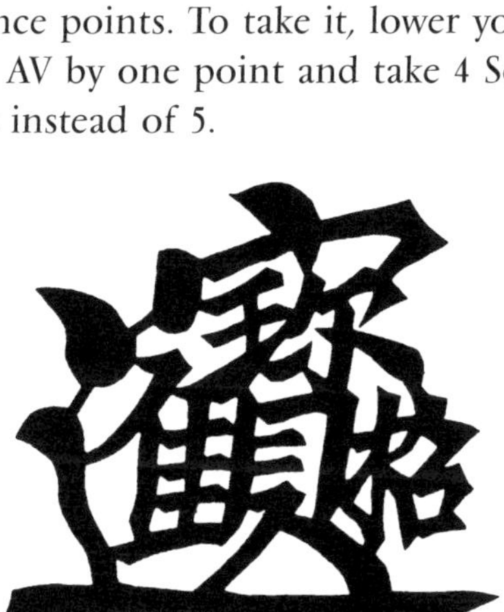

A Note on Gun Powers

Most Gun schticks translate perfectly well to bows, crossbows and slings, with one modification. Both Guns Blazing does not let you fire two bows. Rather, you can nock and fire two arrows at a time. There is also a new schtick, only usable with Bows:

Versatile Ammo

By spending 1 schtick, you guarantee that you never run out of ammo for your bow or crossbow. With 2 schticks, you will always have the best arrow or crossbow bolt for cool archery tricks: y-headed arrows for cutting ropes, grappling hook arrows, arrows that bite into rock or wood, silk rope or cord to tie onto the arrow, etc.

Archer

"I just need one shot."

Most people know archery. Common people learn it to defend their homes against bandits and monsters. The wealthy use it as a sport, and compete with each other in their finely-groomed gardens. But for you, archery is an art form. You have spent years training your eye and hand, learning the stretch of the bow, the feel of the bowstring in your fingers. Perhaps you studied in a monastery, perhaps you were a hired guard or an assassin. Regardless, you knew your place in the world — until now.

Something happened, and you find yourself fighting off both demons and imperial guards. You have found a cause to believe in and people who need your skills. Let your conscience be as true as your aim and you will not fail.

Juncture: 69

Attributes: Bod 5, Chi 0, Mind 5, Ref 6

Add 2 to two different primary attributes. Add 1 to two different secondary attributes.

Skills: Guns (=15)
Info/ [your choice] +2 (7)
Martial Arts +4 (10) [max 13]

Add 5 Skill Bonuses.

Schticks: Signature Weapon plus 4 more Gun schticks

Weapons: 1 bow or crossbow — automatically your Signature Weapon.

Unique Schtick
Flurry of Arrows: As long as your closest enemy is at least 5m away, you gain +2 to initiative.

Quick Schtick Pick
Weapons: Bow
Gun: Carnival of Carnage, Eagle Eye, Fast Draw, Versatile Ammo

Notes: You believe in the absolute superiority of the bow. You will not use firearms — ever.

Wealth Level: Working Stiff

Bandit

"If it makes you feel any better, just consider this a breathing tax."

Nobody starts out wanting to be a bandit. You began life as a farmer, craftsman or merchant. Then disaster struck. A flood destroyed your farm. Imperial taxes drove you into poverty. Perhaps you were the victim of other bandits. In any case, you turned your back on society. You began to live off what you could steal.

After a while, you became quite good. You learned how to fight and how to hide. You learned how to kill. Other bandits now flock to you. Imperial soldiers hunt you. Merchants shudder whenever someone speaks your name.

And yet, you find yourself returning to the very society that you once abandoned. Something draws you there — something you wish to fight for — something you must defend. You have taken the first few steps on a new road. It leads either to your redemption or to your death.

Juncture: 69

Attributes: Body 6, Chi 0 (For=4), Mnd 5, Ref 5

Add 2 to any two primary attributes.

Skills: Martial Arts +4 (9) [Max 13]
Guns +2 (7) [Max 12]
Deceit +2 (7)
Intrusion +2 (7)
Leadership +2 (7)
Info/[previous occupation] +4 (9)

Add 5 Skill Bonuses.

Schticks: 2 Gun schticks
Weapons: 5

Unique Schtick

Lead Mooks: After digging around the unsightly parts of town, you can gather a group of mooks who are willing to fight for you — for a nominal fee, of course. Make a Leadership roll. The difficulty (between 3 and 10) is based on how well you know the area, and how much money you are offering. You gain the Outcome in mooks. They will loyally follow you for one week.

Quick Schtick Pick

Weapons: sling, concealed dagger, staff-sword, crossbow, ax
Gun: Eagle Eye, Versatile Ammo

Wealth Level: Rich

Taoist Wizard

"If you can't trust your own eyes, what can you trust?"

You are a master of illusion and a dabbler in either Fu powers or other arcane arts. Though most of your kind prefer to live like hermits, you have stepped into the real world — into the secret war. Perhaps you were drawn into the battle while trying to help a group of local villagers. Perhaps you wish to save someone or redeem someone. Perhaps the war just hit a little too close to home. In any case, now that you're here you're unlikely to return to your quiet mountainside.

The Lotus and Ascended are your enemies. The Lotus wish to oppress the people of your homeland, while the Ascended will eventually drive magic from the land.

Juncture: 69

Attributes: Bod 5, Chi 5 (Mag=8),
Mnd 5, Ref 5

Add 2 to one primary attribute, 2 points to one secondary attribute.

Skills: Info/Taoism +4 (9)
Martial Arts (=13)
Sorcery (=14)

Add 4 Skill Bonuses.

Schticks: Influence, plus 2 Sorcery or 2 Fu powers.

Unique Schtick

Taoist Trickery: You gain +2 AV on all Influence checks, but -2 on all other Sorcery checks, other than Divination

Quick Schtick Pick

Influence, Friend of Darkness, Dark's Soft Whisper

Wealth Level: Any

APPENDIX C

A Cold Watery Grave

Premise: While visiting America, land of the freak and home of the wacko, the PCs keep stumbling into crazed postal workers, snipers, and rednecks on shooting sprees.

The Twist: A demon has made a deal for his renegade Lotus master that requires the PCs' souls, to be obtained through an elaborate deception.

The Climax: The PCs join forces with the Lotus and the imperial army of 69 A.D. China in an assault on a chi-rich temple.

BACKSTORY

Mang Ri began his career as an insignificant sorcerer. For years, he watched younger members of the Lotus advance while his position never changed. He had power. He understood the use of magic. But he remained small-minded and overly cautious. Regardless of the task, he performed his duty as expected — but never achieved anything noteworthy.

Then things changed. One night Mang Ri woke to find a small, ghostly demon hovering over his bed. Reacting out of fright, he lashed out with a ball of magical energy and trapped the demon. Then he laughed as he watched the now-helpless beast hammer against the magical bubble with its wispy, wraith-like hands.

In exchange for his freedom, the demon offered Mang Ri important information. Several rebels had entered Lo-yang intending to destroy the town's central grain stores. The Demon, named **Five Pains,** helped Mang Ri plan a counterattack timed for optimum drama. Mang Ri walked in just as the rebels set their fires. Within seconds, he incapacitated the rebels and saved the grain. The Petals immediately transferred Mang Ri into the Fire Division. He dreamed of gaining glory, of earning honors and titles, but soon slipped back into his old habits. For two years he slogged through mediocre dependability, and earned only the disappointment of his masters.

Desperate, he summoned Five Pains. The demon readily suggested a deal. He would serve Mang Ri, guaranteeing a prosperous career. In exchange, Mang Ri would help Five Pains escape his demonic masters and give him sanctuary on Earth. Following Five Pains' suggestions, Mang Ri won victory after victory against the Lotus's foes. He earned many honors: The Thorn of Fire, Order of the Screaming Pit, and even the Mark of the Lotus. Soon the Petals advanced him into the Water division and assigned him to the **Temple of Falling Dreams,** a powerful feng shui site along the Empire's Western frontier.

Anyone attuned to the Temple of Falling Dreams gains powers over the sleep of others. They can either bring pleasant and peaceful dreams or they can instill nightmares — particularly nightmares of falling deaths.

A Demonic Plot

Five Pains' capture was no accident — he arranged the entire scene just to get close to Mang Ri. He hopes to use the foolish sor-

Before using the powers granted by the Temple of Falling Dreams, an attuned character must perform a two-hour cleansing ritual. During this ritual they must state their target's name, birth date, and birth time, and then make a Sorcery check against the target's Willpower. If successful, they can either grant a sound night of sleep or inflict horrible nightmares. The target of a pleasant night's rest will find that he or she can operate normally after only four hours of sleep. On the other hand, the target of nightmares will wake up screaming. The target will find it impossible to sleep for a number of hours equal to half the Sorcery check's Outcome. Suffering from sleep deprivation can cause impairment (a -1 AV penalty) at the GM's discretion.

cerer to escape from the Underworld, but not just into a temporary sanctuary. He plans to trick Mang Ri into taking his place in hell. Unfortunately, Five Pain's demonic lord placed two conditions on this exchange. First, Mang Ri needs to agree to it, at least indirectly. Second, Mang Ri must die in battle. To achieve these goals, Five Pains served Mang Ri loyally, letting the sorcerer grow dependent upon him. When Mang Ri ascended to the Temple of Falling Dreams, Five Pains decided to act.

He told Mang Ri that his demonic lord was tracking him down, and that soon he would be dragged back to the Underworld. Desperate for Five Pains' continued advice and support, Mang Ri foolishly promised that he would do anything to prevent Five Pains from returning to the Underworld. This promise was what Five Pains needed; bound in this way, Mang Ri's soul would take Five Pains' place in the Underworld when the time came.

With Mang Ri's agreement in place, Five Pains moved to the next step. Each time Gao Zhang sent for taxes or assistance from Mang Ri, Five Pains sat at his shoulder, whispering doubts. "They expect too much from us. They drive us too hard. And what have they given us? Nothing!" Mang Ri, feeling the pinch on his purse, readily agreed. Soon he began to resist Gao Zhang's authority. He turned away tax collectors empty-handed. He also began to hoard the Temple's chi, using its power to pursue his own goals.

Meanwhile, Five Pains arranged a side deal with **Horns of Fire,** a demonic advisor to Gao Zhang. Horns of Fire agreed to prod Gao into attacking and killing the rebellious Mang Ri. In exchange, Horns of Fire demanded the souls of several individuals who were troubling his master — specifically, the PCs. Already their short career as secret warriors has earned them the enmity of Hell, and Horns of Fire knows that they will only become a growing problem. So Gao Zhang increased his pressure, while Mang Ri increased his rebellion. As tensions rapidly approached a climax, Five Pains talked to Mang Ri once more.

He told Mang Ri that Gao Zhang would soon attack, and would surely crush Mang Ri and the Temple of Falling Dreams — unless they got help. Five Pains knew where it could be found. He told Mang Ri about **General Hong Lei's Sword** — an ancient artifact buried in the great general's tomb. Archeologists in the contemporary juncture recovered the blade and it currently circles the globe in a traveling exhibit of Chinese burial treasures. Five Pains promised that with the sword, Mang Ri could defeat any force Gao

General Hong Lei's Sword

During the Warring States period, General Hong Lei was a warlord feared throughout the subcontinent. With his flaming two-handed sword he led his army to ten thousand victories. This blade became the symbol of his power. In his hands it cut through stone and acted as a beacon for his forces. No matter how chaotic the battle became, they could always see him cutting a clean path through the enemy lines. Normally, the sword inflicts Strength +5 damage and acts as a Signature Weapon (+3 damage, cannot be destroyed or casually lost). However, if the wielder calls out Hong Lei's name then the sword will burst into scarlet flames. The damage increases by an additional +2 (to a total of Strength +10), and the sword can cut through stone or metal as a stunt. The flame power only works once per twenty-four hours, and only lasts an hour.

might send. Five Pains further offered to punch a hole through the Netherworld, allowing Mang Ri to enter the contemporary juncture without going through the Lotus-guarded gates.

Needless to say, Mang Ri agreed — and the die was cast.

ABOUT THIS ADVENTURE

This adventure makes extensive use of the Lotus and the 69 juncture. After witnessing a series of bizarre attacks in the contemporary juncture, the PCs uncover the nefarious plot of a renegade Lotus sorcerer. They attack his contemporary base and then follow him into the 69 juncture. There, they join forces with the Eaters of the Lotus (yes, the Lotus) and lay siege to the renegade in his Temple of Falling Dreams.

This adventure assumes that the PCs have in some way angered the Lotus. This isn't exactly hard to do, of course. If your PC group hasn't yet crossed paths with the Lotus, it's strongly recommended that you save this adventure until this has happened.

In addition, the contemporary portion of this adventure takes place in a generic American city. The exact location is not important and the details are easily convertible, allowing you to place it in any medium-to-large urban area. It is fairly important that America be the setting, however, as a number of American cultural quirks are used. Transplanting it to a city in another country is possible, but you'll need to do some tinkering to de-Americanize that part of the storyline.

Five Pains needs to kill at least three PCs to meet his agreement with Horns of Fire. He'll try to kill at least one PC in every encounter, though of course his chances of this aren't so hot. Primarily, this means he'll pick one PC to beat up on in each encounter and focus his attacks on that PC as much as possible.

GMC NOTES

Here are descriptions of the main GM characters in the story:

FIVE PAINS

Five Pains is a cunning and malevolent demon — but aren't they all? He has successfully manipulated the Lotus sorcerer Mang Ri into serving him while believing that it's the other way around. If all goes well with his current plan, Mang Ri will take Five Pains' place in Hell and Five Pains will be free to roam the Earth. He dislikes direct combat and prefers to get others to do his fighting for him — or at least their bodies!

MANG RI

Mang Ri is an idiot. Despite being a reasonably well-respected Lotus sorcerer and master of the Temple of Falling Dreams, he's really just a below-average buffoon. Luckily for Mang Ri, his demonic servant Five Pains is there to tell him what to do. Unluckily for Mang Ri, Five Pains is about to betray him.

While Mang Ri may well be a buffoon, he's still a potent sorcerer. He's not a coward, and won't hesitate to kill when needed.

GETTING STARTED

One of the PCs has an uncle named Jao Pen who immigrated to the United States and started a Chinese restaurant. For years, Jao Pen has begged the PC to visit but you never had the time. Until now. The Prof suspects that Li Li's (Jao Pen's restaurant) is a minor feng shui site and she has asked the PCs to investigate. After landing in America, Jao Pen meets them at the gate. He is a plump, grandfatherly man with a friendly grin. At his side stands an attractive young woman — his daughter Mo Szu.

If the PCs aren't allied with the Prof, it's no big deal. Develop another pretext to get the PCs to Jao Pen's. Perhaps Jao Pen knows a little about the Secret War and has been told by a geomancer that his restaurant is a bona fide feng shui site. Perhaps he's being harassed by local gangsters. Perhaps he has a secret inheritance for the PC related to the PC's dramatic hook. One way or another, the PCs shouldn't be hard-pressed to go to America.

Five Pains, demonic manipulator

Sample Dialogue: "Oh no, master, I am sure they will not betray you. They told me so personally!"

Distinguishing Features: Five Pains is a ghost-like demon. His size varies depending on his need but generally remains between 30 cm and 3 m. This has no effect on his game stats. It merely aids his Deceit or Intimidation checks.

Attributes: Body 7, Chi 5 (For 2), Mnd 8, Ref 10

Skills: Creature Power 18, Deceit 15, Martial Arts 15, Intimidation 12

Creature Schticks: Body Borrow, Flight, Insubstantial, Regeneration (x2)

Base Damage: 8 (hands)

Unique Schtick

Empowerment: Five Pains can empower anyone he possesses if he can make a Creature Power check versus the target's Willpower. If successful, he can then allocate a number of skill bonuses, attribute bonuses, or schticks equal to the outcome. Skill bonuses allocated cannot exceed 8. Attribute points allocated cannot exceed 8. Schticks must be appropriate to the possessed character. These can include any types of schticks that the character already possesses or generic schticks for their juncture. For the 69 and 1850 junctures, use Fu schticks. For the contemporary or 2056 junctures, use Gun schticks. (In this scenario, Five Pains has granted or improved the Gun skill and many Gun schticks of various possessed GMCs, which have already been added to their stats.) **Note:** the Empowerment schtick only works on unnamed characters, temporarily changing them into named characters for game purposes.

Punch Passages: Five Pains can create temporary passageways through the Netherworld. See the nearby description of Punch Passages for more details.

Mang Ri, renegade eunuch sorcerer

Attributes: Bod 4, Chi 0 (mag 9), Mnd 5, Ref 6

Skills: Deceit 9, Info/Lotus Politics 7, Intrusion 9, Leadership 7, Sorcery 18

Schticks: Blast (fire, conjured weapons, transmutation), Heal, Influence, Movement, Summoning, Weather

New Schtick

Punch Passages: A few powerful supernatural creatures, such as Five Pains, have the ability to punch short passageways through the Netherworld. These passages form a direct connection between two open junctures. They do not lead into the Netherworld as a whole. They also typically measure less than five hundred meters from gateway to gateway. Punch Passages last from one week to several months. No one knows what happens to people caught in the passageway when it collapses. Some believe that they fall into a random time period. Others think they shift into the Netherworld proper — or maybe even another dimension entirely. However, most assume that they simply cease to exist.

DEMON RUNS AMUCK

Soon, the Hillside Museum of History will open the traveling exhibit *Jade and Clay: A Look into Ancient China.* While Mang Ri waits impatiently for General Hong Lei's Sword to arrive, he gathers a small army of brainwashed goons. Meanwhile, Five Pains locates the promised souls (the PCs) and draws them into his web. The following encounters can take place in any order. It's recommended that all of the PCs be present at each encounter, so that no one has to sit out a combat.

Ambitious GMs with large groups of players could attempt to split up the PCs among the three encounters and run them simultaneously — but your brain will probably explode if you try this.

Note: While each encounter has its own complications, one common thread links them all: the PCs will need to split their attention between protecting innocent bystanders and attacking the possessed assailant. Five Pains will try to kill at least one PC in this encounter, but he won't put himself at risk to do this; he knows he has plenty more chances. Regardless of what else happens, Five Pains must survive these encounters. Once the host body dies (or the PCs manage to attack him directly), he will flee.

GOING POSTAL

The game begins as the PCs settle into Li Li's for a terrific meal served by Jao Pen. Friends of Jao Pen's daughter Mo soon stop by — a group of twenty-something men and women. (Yes, these can provide romantic interests for unattached PCs if desired.) However, no one has a chance to get too relaxed. Jao Pen finds a note in his mail saying that the post office is holding a package for him, waiting for a signature. It is a shipment of green tea that he special-ordered from Hong Kong. Eager to examine the tea, Jao Pen asks Mo and the PCs to pick up the package before the post office closes, since he's got a busy crowd at the restaurant and will be tied up all afternoon.

The main branch of the post office is a large, blocky building nestled in the heart of downtown. Double front doors open into a small foyer. To the right sit several alcoves filled with post-office boxes and stamp-vending machines. On the left, another set of doors opens into the main room. A long counter bisects this room. A dozen postal employees work on one side, surrounded by boxes, mail bags, and bulky governmental office equipment. On the other, five lines of customers wait impatiently.

While the characters stand in line, Five Pains seizes the opportunity. Borrowing the body of Greg Osborne, a disgruntled ex-postal employee, he buys a 12-gauge shotgun, hides it in a gym bag, and enters the Post Office. The PCs should attempt a Police, Detective, or Perception check (Difficulty 10). Anyone succeeding will notice Greg enter the building and look around furtively. Everyone else remains blissfully unaware until his shotgun goes "KA-CHINK."

Greg shoots a patron just to get everyone's attention (the attack automatically succeeds,

Greg Osborne, possessed, unemployed mailman

Attributes: Bod 5, Chi 0, Mnd 4, Ref 6
Skills: Guns 14, Tgh 12, Intimidation 8
Schticks: Carnival of Carnage (x4), Hair-Trigger Neck Hairs, Lightning Reload (x3)
Damage: 13 (kills unnamed characters with an Outcome of 3 or more).
Note: Shots fired at inanimate objects cost 1 shot. Greg will squeeze them off as necessary to keep the scene interesting and dynamic.

Generic Bystanders

Sample Dialogue: "Look out! He's got a gun!"
Attributes: Bod 5, Chi 0, Mnd 4, Ref 4
Skills: Dodge 7
Unique Schtick
Stampede: When attacked, bystanders will begin to panic. This will typically result in a stampede. PCs caught in the stampede will need to make a Martial Arts check. Unless their Action Result exceeds 12, the crowd will knock them down and trample them. They lose all remaining shots this sequence and take 8 points of damage. An Action Result of 8–12 will allow the PC to prevent this damage but they still lose the shots.
Notes: Bystanders excel at screaming and running about in confused masses. In general, they will make a liability of themselves — hopefully endangering the characters in the process.

mortally wounding the victim). Then he begins to shout: "You thought you could get away with it, didn't you? You thought you could just throw me aside. That I'd just disappear. Well, we'll see who gets 'terminated' now!" Greg continues to shoot up the building — largely targeting mail bags, packages and such. In the resulting explosions, half-burnt letters and packing popcorn fills the air. He also shoots anyone who approaches. If multiple characters try to engage him, he shouts, "Stay back!" and blows away another customer or employee.

- An exploding mail bag creates a temporary cloud of envelopes. This can blind characters and provide cover.
- The P.O. Box alcoves provide ideal cover. Of course, the more intelligent bystanders will also realize this and lead the stampede in that direction.
- An errant shot hits one of the stamp machines. Coins spill out onto the already slippery floor, making footing hazardous (-1 AV to any acrobatic stunts).
- A PC notices that one of the packages is ticking — completely coincidental mad bomber! A sequence later, an errant shot strikes it. The resulting explosion takes out half the building (Damage 12 to everyone inside).

POWER IN THE TOWER

"We're gonna cream you losers!" That's how you start this scene off. Just bellow that at the players without *any* set-up whatsoever, and *then* tell them that they are playing beach volleyball against a bunch of steroidal jocks. WKIZ, a local pop radio station, has set up three artificial beach volleyball courts in the city's courthouse square. Jao Pen is on hand with a food booth for Li Li's from which he serves tasty treats to the sweaty crowd.

Three-person teams compete for a $500 prize; any extra PCs are on the sidelines, knocking back a cold beer and jeering at their friends. Mo Szu and her friends (who were eliminated in earlier rounds) are also on hand, cheering wildly. A WKIZ remote facility broadcasts from the scene while street performers and vendors mill about the gathering crowd.

It's the start of the finals, and the PCs have done well. The other team is about to serve just as the scene begins. Don't give the PCs any time to think about this; just get right into it and serve the ball.

Rules: The game is run similarly to combat. Everyone makes an Initiative check — this does not determine the order in which they act. Rather, it simply gives each character a number of shots to spend that sequence. To begin the sequence, one person serves (Martial Arts check, shot cost 3). A character on the other side then blocks the shot (Martial Arts Check, Difficulty equaling the previous Action Result, shot cost 1). A different character on the same side must then spike the ball back (yet another Martial Arts check, shot cost 3). Someone on the opposing team tries to block it... and so it goes. Once you run out of shots, you can no longer act — either to block or to spike. One side scores when the opponents either fail to block or are unable to spike the ball. These games use typical volleyball scoring. You only gain points while serving. As long as you continue to score, you continue to serve. Once the other side scores against you, they gain the serve. For time's sake, these games are played to 6. You must win by at least 2 points.

The courthouse square consists of a park and band shell surrounded on all sides by trendy shops. The city courthouse sits squarely at one end. Its clock tower rises well above all other structures, giving it a good view of the surrounding area. After Five Pains' possession, courthouse office secretary Marsha Thompson politely excuses herself from work and climbs the tower. She locks the only door accessing the stairway, breaking the key inside the lock. Then she bars the trapdoor at the top.

If the players are enjoying the volleyball game, play it through to the end. Make sure and do a lot of interaction with the opposing team, so you and the players can trade insults as the ball flies back and forth. If the players aren't into it, just do a couple serves and then let the shooting start.

At whatever point you think is good, Marsha Thompson blows away the volleyball judge, bringing the game to a bloody halt and kicking off some real competition. As the crowd screams, more shots ring out; Marsha shoots at bystanders, cars, windows, and whatever else she feels like. It doesn't take long to realize that the shots are coming from the courthouse clock tower. At least a couple of shots will be fired at a single PC, as Five Pains tries to wax him for good and appease Horns of Fire.

ACCESSING THE TOWER

The PCs should have trouble getting to Marsha. She is crouched in the small room that houses the clock's bells. Firing from narrow, slit-like windows, she has 90% cover (+6 to her Dodge). Flying is an option for characters with appropriate schticks — of course, this makes them a prime target, without any cover. Climbing is also relatively easy (Difficulty of 8), and Marsha will not notice climbers until they reach the windows. Of course, once she sees them she will shoot them off the wall. Regardless, the windows are pairs of narrow, open slits too small for anyone to squeeze past. The PCs must hang onto the tower while attacking through the slits. This gives both the PCs and Marsha 25% cover (+1 Dodge).

Most PCs, however, will need to use the stairs. The downstairs door is locked and the lock is broken. Furthermore, as a heavy fire door, it requires considerable force to break down. The door has a Dodge of 0 and a Toughness of 10. Alternatively, PCs could target the lock (Dodge of 6, Toughness of 5). Like named characters, once these take 35 points of damage they will make death checks (using their Toughness). If they fail, the door falls open or the lock blows out.

Upstairs, the task becomes more complicated. The stairs end in a small landing. A permanently attached wooden ladder reaches up to the overhead trapdoor. This door opens upwards and has been barred from above. Because of the positioning, only one PC can attack from the ladder at a time. He will also have a -2 AV modifier due to poor footing and general awkwardness. Still, this door is weaker than the one downstairs. It has a Dodge of 0 and a Toughness of 7.

- Marsha shoots the driver of a vehicle. Of course, the dead body steps on the gas and veers toward either the PCs or a group of unsuspecting bystanders (usually including small children and infants).
- As part of her preparations, Marsha could booby-trap the bottom door. Once the PCs force it open a small bomb explodes. Anyone within 1m of the door takes 20 points of damage. Others nearby take 10. This also destroys the bottom 15 feet of the stairway. **Note:** You should probably limit yourself to one explosion in these

First Round, unnamed volleyball players

Attributes: Bod 5, Chi 0, Mnd 5, Ref 5
Skills: Martial Arts 10 (for volleyball only)
Note: Each round, increase the team's Ref by +1 and the Martial Arts by +2

Marsha Thompson, secretary and possessed NRA gun buff

Attributes: Bod 4, Tgh 11, Chi 0, Mnd 5, Ref 6
Skills: Guns 14
Schticks: Carnival of Carnage (x2), Eagle Eye, Lightning Reload (x3)
Damage: 13 (Kills unnamed characters with an Outcome of 3 or more).

introductory scenes. Use either the mail bomb at the post office or the booby-trap bomb, not both.

- A car crash catches a nearby building on fire. The resulting inferno traps small children in a daycare center on the third floor.
- The clock tower's bells begin to ring. Everyone inside is stunned (loses a number of shots equal to 15 minus their Toughness). Furthermore, everyone is temporarily deaf. They hear nothing but ringing for a full five minutes.

DRIVE-THROUGH SHOOTING

A redneck, a big ol' pickup truck, and a glass-front mall. The result should be obvious. The Hamilton Galleria is a T-shaped, two-story mall. The glass front and main entrance open to a wide promenade which leads to the back hallway. Escalators and stairs stand in the open center of the promenade. On the second floor, narrower walkways hug the edge forming a continual balcony. The stores here target elite shoppers. They are almost universally trendy and high-priced.

The PCs are at the mall, shopping with Mo and her friends. Take this opportunity to mercilessly lampoon American shopping malls, if you feel like it. Have costumed characters rampaging through the halls, passing out coupons and hugging children, while jugglers toss plastic balls full of dollar bills around ("Money is fun!"). If you need a better reason to be there, bring Jao Pen along, too; he's considering opening up a fast-food version of Li Li's here at the mall and he's scouting out the location.

The action starts as they start to leave the mall. A rusted-out red pickup with "Hoss" painted on the doors drives up the front stairs and through the glass wall. Flying glass scatters throughout the promenade. Characters must make a Martial Arts check (Shot Cost 1, Difficulty 8) to avoid taking 10 points of damage from the flying shards. After driving his pickup through the front of the mall, Billy-Bob Williams will continue to squeal through shop fronts and the wide promenades ("Hey, the new model cars are in."), shooting his Colt Anaconda out the window with his left hand. Once he spots the PCs, he'll ignore the bystanders for the most part and just try to grind the PCs beneath his mighty wheels.

Billy-Bob, possessed redneck

Attributes: Bod 7, Tgh 13, Chi 0, Mnd 4, Ref 5
Skills: Drive 8, Gun 14
Schticks: Carnival of Carnage (x4), Lightning Reload (x3), Signature Weapon (Hoss the Truck)
Damage: 20 (truck), 11 (pistol)
Note: The truck offers Billy-Bob 75% cover (+4). Also, it acts as his signature weapon. No matter how much damage it takes, it will continue to run — somehow. Additionally, Carnival of Carnage schticks works equally well for the truck or the gun, allowing Billy-Bob to mow over large clusters of shoppers.

- During the fight, Billy-Bob inflicts severe structural damage to the mall. A portion of the second floor begins to groan, then buckles and collapses. Anyone standing on it must make a successful Martial Arts check (1 Shot, Difficulty 8) or take 15 points of damage. Those underneath must make a Martial Arts check (Difficulty 12) or take 20 points.
- A group of five 12-year-old gang members decide to get into the action. Just shooting for kicks, they are not too particular about their targets.

AFTERMATH

Sometime during these encounters, the PCs need to discover the demonic possession behind the attacks. This will probably result from their continued investigation. In every case, friends, family, and co-workers will swear that the attackers acted out of character. Greg Osborne was a pacifist. He never touched a gun in his life. Marsha Thompson, while an avid gun collector and active NRA member, continually advocated personal responsibility and gun awareness. She even taught gun safety classes for hunters and sports shooters. Finally, despite his explosive and violent temper, Billy-Bob's friends admit that he is a hopeless fighter. In brawls, he has a notorious glass jaw. His friends also swear that he could not shoot a target if he placed the barrel of his gun against the bullseye.

Magical inquiries reveal hazy answers — a hint of the sinister, combined with a touch of the supernatural. (For example, Divination (Revelation) checks will reveal a twisted, black aura around the possessed combatant.) An I Ching reading gives the following: Ku — Work on What Has Been Spoiled. The symbol Ku represents a bowl, in whose contents worms are breeding.

I Ching's Judgment:
Work on What Has Been Spoiled
Has supreme success.
It furthers one to cross the great water.
Before the starting point, three days.
After the starting point, three days.

There are also two lines in motion.

Six at the beginning:
Setting right what has been spoiled by the father. If there is a son,
No blame rests upon the departed father.
Danger. In the end good fortune.

Nine at the Top:
He does not serve kings and princes,
Sets himself higher goals.

The reference to crossing great water refers to the upcoming journey into the past. As the "Before... three days. After... three days." lines suggest, the initial attacks mark the beginning of a larger problem. More will come. The first moving line suggests the demon's presence — hinting at an outside influence. The second moving line refers to Five Pain's goals. It also suggests the supernatural influences present.

Unnamed Baby Gangstas, yuppie rebels

Attributes: Bod 4, Chi 0, Mnd 4, Ref 4
Skills: Guns 8
Damage: 8

If the characters manage to capture one of the attackers, Five Pains will abandon his host, throwing the body into temporarily unconsciousness. When the host recovers, he or she remembers nothing about the incident.

Finally, if the PCs still don't get it, Five Pains will possess the body of an elderly homeless person and perform the crazy/wise mystic act. "You have seen many unusual things, yes? Yes... yes. But you don't yet understand them. There is more here than you realize. A darkness that swallows the land." He pauses, looking the PCs in the eye. "An ancient evil has returned. You must stop it, stop it or we are all doomed." Then the homeless person collapses. When he recovers, he likewise remembers nothing about the event.

ASCENDED ATTENTION

If the PCs use either magic or creature powers, they are likely to attract unwanted attention from the Ascended. However, the Pledged operatives will proceed cautiously — hoping to build a strong pool of information before making their move. This will undoubtedly begin with a visit from FBI Special Agent Benjamin Franklin Smith. Smith isn't really an FBI agent; he works for whatever secret government agency you want him to. He just poses as an FBI agent to head off tricky questions.

He will interview the PCs regarding their involvement in the attack. Any PCs who are involved in more than one attack will receive special attention as Smith wants to know why he continually finds them in the line of fire.

Furthermore, if the PCs used any obviously

supernatural abilities, Smith begins to ask leading questions. He will pretend to dismiss any supernatural claims as delusions or otherwise-explainable phenomena — however, he really wants to uncover the depth of the PCs' power. Depending on the PCs' actions during the fights and their behavior during the interview, Smith may arrest them on any number of charges — from murder to conspiracy. However, if Smith believes that they possess supernatural abilities he will send a squad of Men in Black to deal with the situation. Be careful when introducing this subplot. It can provide excitement between attacks, but it should not derail the main story. However, it can provide the groundwork for a future Ascended adventure.

Smith can turn up again if you like in future adventures, even in foreign countries. He'll always have I.D. showing that he's a representative of whatever governmental law enforcement organization that has jurisdiction in the situation at hand. If he recognizes the PCs, he'll give them a big smile and pretend they've never met, just to annoy them.

Benjamin Franklin Smith, transformed fox

Attributes: Bod 5, Chi 7 (For 6), Mnd 8 (Wil 6), Ref 7
Skills: Guns 15, Martial Arts 13, Police 12
Schticks: Embezzle, Mockery, Swindle (x2)
Notes: Ben Smith has worked as an Ascended pledge within the U.S. government for five years. He specializes in "debunking" supernatural claims. In other words, he invents rational explanations for the inexplicable, then disposes of the sorcerers or supernatural creatures involved so that his non-pledged superiors in the government don't look too closely at the Secret War. Once the PCs have attracted Ben's attention, he will continue to keep a close eye on them — waiting for them to make a mistake.

Men in Black, elite mooks

Attributes: Bod 7, Chi 0, Mnd 6, Ref 8
Skills: Guns 11, Intimidation 11, Intrusion 11
Unique Schtick
Relentless Reality: All schticks have a –2 AV when used against the Men in Black.
Damage: 10 (pistol)
Notes: These dark-suited pledged operatives act as hit men for the Ascended. They will always appear in superior numbers (equal to the number of PCs +2). They also time their attacks so that the target characters are alone — leaving no witnesses.

BETWEEN SCENES

The PCs should spend some time between scenes roleplaying ordinary life (with the occasional trip to the hospital). Give them a chance to relax and interact with Jao, Mo, and the other GMCs. Li Li's Restaurant can be a feng shui site if you wish; if so, the PCs might be concerned about the Secret War exploding in Jao Pen's kitchen. They might want to talk to him about acquiring an interest in the restaurant so that they can attune to the site and protect it. However, do not let the story slow down. As soon as the game begins to lag, jump forward into the next action scene.

One particular area in which you might foster some between-scene interest is with Mo Szu. She'll presumably have seen the PCs in action, and she may get very intrigued. She can pester the PCs with questions about their powers, about what's going on, and telling Jao Pen how brave they all are. Potentially, Mo could join the Secret War in some fashion; maybe the PCs can help her attune to the feng shui site at the restaurant and make her an ally. Play up Mo's interest in these matters, and don't let her come off like an airhead; she's a bright young woman who'd love the chance to save the world, or at least the restaurant.

Another possibility is to have Jao Pen be fully cognizant of the Secret War. Perhaps he was a warrior in his youth, and has kept it a secret all these years out of a desire for a quiet life. When things start going crazy, he could reveal his secret past and suggest demonic possession as the cause for the shootings.

THE PROF

If the PCs are allied with the Prof, they will probably try to call home and ask for advice or assistance. The Prof will eagerly listen to their story, but will not send any support unless the situation becomes more serious. Still, she will ask them to keep her informed.

NEWS AT 11:00

Once the characters realize that something strange is behind these attacks, the following story hits the news.

Last night, just after midnight, several armed robbers broke into the Hillside Museum of History. Though extensive damage is reported, nothing was stolen. A raging gunfight occurred between the robbers and the museum security, ending when the police arrived and the robbers fled.

According to the guards, the robbers seemed interested in just one item — a 2,500 year-old Chinese sword. The sword was part of *Jade and Clay: A Look into Ancient China,* a traveling exhibit due to open tomorrow.

The museum curator, Mary Swiss, says that although the sword is priceless, it is not the type of artifact that generally catches a thief's eye. Many other displays contained jewels and gold, items much easier to sell.

The police echo this confusion regarding the robbers' motivations. According to Commissioner Jake Williams, the robbers' methods seem to imply a gang operation. However, no one knows why any gangs would be interested in an ancient sword. Regardless, the Hillside Museum has increased their security during the exhibit's stay. Police officers now supplement the regular guards and the exhibit will open as scheduled.

This should be sufficient to get the characters interested in the sword. However, if they hesitate then Five Pains will perform the ancient mystic trick again, dropping further clues in their laps (possibly even possessing Jao Pen and giving him ecstatic visions). He suggests that the sword possesses great power — power that could be used for good or evil. From here, the characters can proceed in two basic directions. They can try to work with the police, or they can just case the museum and wait.

THE POLICE

Any attempt to gain additional information will be met with stiff resistance, unless the PCs have a valid reason to become involved. If one of the characters is a local cop, he could easily gain access to the police reports and might be able to convince his supervisors into adding the party to the museum's new security detail. Similarly, a Hong Kong police officer may be able to trick his way in by claiming that his government sent him to investigate the attack and protect the artifacts.

In any case, the police suspect a new gang named the Mongols. They spotted two known Mongols during the firefight and counted a half-dozen combatants total. However, the gang appears to be led by an unknown elderly Chinese man. This stranger dressed oddly. He wore elaborate silk robes and an intricate headpiece.

Sergeant Peters, one of the officers on the scene, reported, "Yeah, looked like he just stepped out of the exhibit. Weird old guy. He shattered the case holding the sword, and grabbed it. Then, I don't know. I tried to shoot him, but someone came up from behind and knocked him to the ground. I didn't get a good look — but the guy was dressed in a gauzy-gray outfit — almost looked like smoke. Anyway, when the old man fell, he dropped the sword. It clattered toward us. He tried to come after it, but Johnson winged him. Then they all ran."

THE WAITING GAME

Having failed on his first attempt (thanks to Five Pains' meddling) Mang Ri will try again. The PCs might sign on to the Museum's new security, or they might just case the place. On the other hand, the PCs could visit the exhibit just to look at this mysterious blade. That, of course, would be an ideal time for Mang Ri to attack.

In any case, at least one PC should be present when the Mongols return. The second attack will occur during business hours. Mang Ri and twelve Mongol mooks will enter the museum with the regular patrons. (They will be dressed in normal clothes with no gang insignia or other oddities immediately visible.) After winding their way through the various exhibits, they will approach General Hong Lei's sword. Mang Ri will shatter the glass case again, grabbing the blade. He will then use all the magic at his disposal to escape — including flying through a ceiling sunroof. Meanwhile, his mooks will whip out submachine guns and create a diversion. Regardless of anything else, Mang Ri must escape with the sword.

Police and Museum Guards, legally employed mooks

Attributes: Bod 5, Chi 0, Mnd 5, Ref 5
Skills: Guns 8
Damage: 10 (Pistol)
Notes: Start the fight with two guards in the room. Six others are scattered throughout the building, and two will arrive each sequence. If the fight lasts longer than five sequences, more police begin to show up at the rate of four per sequence until the fight ends. To simplify the battle, you can divide the Mongols into two groups — those fighting the police and those fighting the PCs. Subtract the number of police from the number of Mongols they face. Then make an open roll and add that to the result. If the result is positive, one of the police dies. A negative result kills one of the Mongols.

Mongols, magically controlled mooks

Attributes: Bod 6, Chi 0, Mnd 4, Ref 6
Skills: Drive (motorcycles) 10, Guns 8
Damage: 10 (Uzi)
Notes: The Mongols are easily identified by their black leather jackets, with a painting of a fur-clad Mongol Warrior riding a Harley. They all enter the museum wearing trenchcoats (to hide the calling-card jackets), but will remove them once the fight begins.

COMPLICATIONS

- Yet again, the characters contend with panicked bystanders.
- The police and museum guards mistake the PCs for criminals (possibly a rival gang) and open fire. Of course, if the PCs somehow got work as guards then this does not apply.
- A large Roman statue topples, inflicting 10 points of damage to anyone caught underneath it (Martial Arts action result of 12 or better, 1 Shot).
- A glass display case explodes from gunfire. Flying glass causes 8 points of damage to everyone within 1 meter.
- Remember Special Agent Smith? He decides to show up with some Men in Black...

THE NEXT STEP

With any luck, the PCs incapacitate and capture one of the Mongols. (If nothing else, one of the Mongols dropped by the cops or a PC is still alive or is revived by paramedics.) Now free of Mang Ri's influence, he willingly describes their temporary hideout at the Bent-Hartly construction site just south of town.

Failing that, the PCs have several other paths leading to Bent-Hartly. They could follow Mang Ri or an escaping Mongol, or they could spot one of the Mongols the next day and tail him to the sight. Making inquiries among seedy dives will point the PCs in the direction of some toughs affiliated with the Mongols but not part of the gang who can them give them information about their friends' recent strange behavior.

SHOWDOWN

Five Pains' Punch Passage opens into the basement of the Bent-Hartly construction site. Planned as the future location of the Bent-Hartly Tower, the large hotel would have included a three-floor shopping mall and a five-star restaurant. However, two of the original investors pulled out and construction halted due to monetary snafus. For the moment, it remains an abandoned lower shell with thirty floors of scaffolding rising from the middle. Two open elevators give access to these upper regions. Six Mongols patrol the perimeter at all times. Another dozen reside inside. Once alerted by gunfire (or the screams of the dying), they will take a sequence or two to gather their weapons and rush out.

The GM needs to decide if Mang Ri and Five Pains are still around. If the PCs got here shortly after the robbery, they'll be around and ready to tangle. If it's the next day, the pair will have already traveled through the gate — but Five Pains will have secretly left the gate open to allow them to follow. The Mongols will still be around as normal, but after the fight they can tell the PCs that Mang Ri and his weird friend took off through a weird tunnel in the basement.

If Mang Ri and Five Pains are here for the fight, they will try to lure the PCs into the upper regions of the scaffolding. Once there, their flying ability gives them a slight advantage. If the PC head up, the Mongols will, too.

Once Mang Ri takes a point of impairment, he will retreat into the basement and flee through the gate there. Five Pains will try to distract the PCs temporarily and then follow Mang Ri. Again, both must survive. Well-timed Mongol attacks at the moment that the pair flee should facilitate this without being too obvious.

COMPLICATIONS

- The scaffolding provides many steel beams to hide behind, balance on, and so forth. Occasional planking provides some stable footing as long as no one kicks it down or breaks it. There are also ample cables to swing or climb on.
- A Mongol begins using a crane to swing a four-meter steel beam at the PCs (AV 8, Damage 20). There is another crane, if the PCs want it.
- When characters are balanced on the steel beams, any blow that inflicts more Wound Points than the character's Agility will knock him off. He can make a Martial Arts check to catch himself and stop the fall (Shot Cost 1, Difficulty 8). However, unless the character receives an outcome of 5 or better, this will leave him in a compromised position (hanging from his fingertips, clinging to a cable, whatever).

INTO THE NETHER-WORLD

After picking their way back down the scaffolding, the PCs can pursue Mang Ri into the building's basement, only to find him gone. (Alternately, if Mang Ri was already gone then the soundly thrashed Mongols can point the way.) The only exit is a 2m x 1m tunnel dug through the cinder-block wall. The sides of the tunnel look like moist, gray limestone, but they feel warm and somewhat plastic — if the PCs have been to the Netherworld before, it's obvious to them that this is a Netherworld passageway.

If the PCs enter, they discover that the passageway only extends 200m. Stepping out on the other side, they find themselves in subzero temperatures and blizzard-like conditions. Blowing snow reduces visibility to 5m if they are lucky. Gale-force winds seem to claw the warmth away from their bodies. This is a polite clue to go back and get additional supplies. Anyone who ignores it deserves their fate. They will become lost, and the harsh environment will begin to sap their strength. The wind and cold inflicts 10 points of damage per minute — and that does not include potential hazards like falling off an unseen cliff. The PCs should not be sure if this is some strange Netherworld chamber or if the passageway has led directly from the contemporary juncture to some other real-world locale.

Back in the contemporary juncture, the PCs will need to gather supplies. This should include heavy winter clothing, cold-weather camping gear, and miscellaneous supplies; ambitious groups may opt for a snowmobile for each PC and trailer sleds to haul this stuff around. (Potentially, magical solutions to the climatic problems could be found if the PCs are inventive — but since they don't know how far they must travel or how long they will be in those conditions, this is a risky proposition.) The PCs may want to do some reconnoitering of the strange place at the end of the tunnel before deciding just what supplies they should take.

Once properly equipped, the PCs can return to the tunnel and will find that nature no longer presents a serious problem. Though heavy snow still falls, the PCs can see a narrow path cutting its way down the mountainside. The path is wide enough for their snowmobiles — barely. It takes the PCs two full days to reach the bottom using snowmobiles, or four days on foot.

MANDATORY ROPE BRIDGE

Yes, half way down the mountainside the party encounters a rickety rope bridge spanning a 20m wide chasm. The ice-coated boards look badly rotten and the ropes do not seem much better. The chasm is full of mist, leaving the PCs uncertain how far a fall might be — but it's obviously a long way. Each PC needs to make a Fortune roll when attempting to cross the bridge. The Difficulty depends on exactly how they try to cross. Walking requires an AR of -1 or better. Driving a snowmobile or pushing a sled requires an AR of 2. Driving a snowmobile with an attached sled requires an AR of 5. If multiple people try to cross at once, add the total difficulties together with an additional +1 AR for each person after the first. If any of the rolls fail, the bridge collapses. The PC must make a Martial Arts check (Difficulty 8) to grab onto something. Any snowmobile or sled currently on the bridge is lost.

If anyone falls into the chasm, you can give him a chance to grab the flailing ropes or to land on a ledge 30m down in the mist, or you can just let him fall screaming to his doom. That's what chasms are for, after all.

The threat here should be real, and any PCs who die here will count towards the minimum of three that Five Pains needs to kill.

Of course, the bridge is only the first problem. Mang Ri has stationed six of his guards here at a camp on the far side of the bridge. Once half the party crosses the bridge (or the bridge collapses) they will attack.

Combat aside, it is possible that some members of the party (and their supplies) will become stranded on the wrong side of the chasm. It is impossible to predict all the ways PCs may attempt to cross — so we'll just look at one of the more ridiculous ideas. With some work, the stranded characters can build a ramp out of snow and then try to jump a snowmobile across the chasm. For just the snowmobile, this requires a Drive check (Difficulty 10). For the snowmobile and sled, the Difficulty goes up to 13. Other options include using magical flight or fu powers, making some sort of insanely-good martial arts jump, or shooting a grappling hook and rope to the PCs on the far side and then climbing across the chasm while hanging from the line.

THE IMPERIAL ARMY

At the valley bottom, a frozen river cuts through the ground in front of the PCs. To their left, they see the valley widen as the river flows into a large lake. A single island rises out of the center of the lake with a dark temple resting atop it. To the right, the PCs spot several columns of armed men marching their direction — there are hundreds of soldiers here. Two dozen mounted soldiers, obviously from a much earlier time than the contemporary juncture, instantly break off from the main group and ride towards them.

The PCs have two options. If they run, they will head straight into Mang Ri's waiting hands; proceed with the next section ("The Final Assault") except that the PCs do not have the distraction provided by the imperial army. Multiply the number of mooks they face by ten, and have the army attack late in the combat just for fun.

If the PCs wait, the soldiers will surround them and then the sergeant will call out: "Who are you? What are you doing here?" The soldiers are confused by the PCs' strange clothing and appearance, and are particularly

Mang Ri's Guards, ancient mooks

Attributes: Bod 5, Chi 0, Mnd 5, Ref 5
Skills: Martial Arts 9, Gun 8
Damage: 7 (bow), 9 (sword)

Captain Ma Yi, Lotus vassal

Attributes: Bod 8, Chi 4 (For 0), Mnd 5, Ref 7
Skills: Guns 12, Info/Military Tactics 12, Martial Arts 15
Schticks: Armored in Life, Clothed in Life, Walk of a Thousand Steps, Willow Step

Average Imperial Soldier, loyal mooks

Attributes: Bod 6, Chi 0, Mnd 5, Ref 6
Skills: Guns 9, Martial Arts 9
Note: The Imperial Army has roughly five hundred soldiers deployed in this attack.

confused by any snowmobiles that might be present. While showing a mixture of mistrust and fear, they demand that the PCs accompany them back to the main army. If the PCs try to resist, the soldiers attack. Five additional soldiers arrive every sequence until the PCs surrender or stop fighting. The soldiers will then chain the survivors together, taking them back to camp.

In either case, the PCs will be brought before a gilded carriage. Two men step out. The larger wears a military uniform — he is clearly the commander of the army. The other looks like a scholar, dressed in ice-white silk. These are Captain Ma Yi and Fire Thorn Ku Qiao. Though Ma Yi technically controls the army, with Ku Qiao as his advisor, Ku's sorcerous abilities make him the true center of power. Gao Zhang sent Ma Yi and Ku Qiao to kill Mang Ri and dissipate his power structure. Once they realize that the PCs also oppose Mang Ri, they will suggest a truce. If they all work together, they can defeat a mutual annoyance.

It's possible that the PCs could begin fighting the soldiers or even Ma Yi and Ku Qiao and then make an escape, but it's not real likely. A good chunk of the imperial army is here, after all, so the Lotus have a huge supply of mooks to call on. Unless the PCs have supernatural means of escape, they'll probably be fighting until they surrender or are taken down like dogs. Capture by the Lotus is a real possibility, but any PCs who attack an entire army deserve what they get.

THE FINAL ASSAULT

The imperial army marches to the edge of the lake, camping on its shore. That night, everyone hears strange howls echoing from the Temple of Falling Dreams. No one sleeps well as waves of falling nightmares sweep through the camp (though this has no effect in game terms). When dawn comes the army breaks camp, forms into ranks, and prepares for the six-hundred-meter charge across the frozen lake. The PCs take whatever role in the battle they wish.

The temple is a sprawling two-story building. Built to keep out the harsh Tibetan weather, it provides some protection to the inhabitants — but it was not built for war. Mang Ri keeps fifty archers at the windows and takes another fifty soldiers and a half-dozen demonic warriors down to meet the army. Leading the first charge, Mang Ri activates General Hong Lei's flaming sword. Once he receives his first point of impairment he retreats to the temple, leaving the demons and troops to cover his escape. He then summons a blizzard, hoping that nature will drive off his enemy.

Since the imperial army distracts much of Mang Ri's force, the PCs only need to fight past 8 mooks before facing the sorcerer (or

Fire Thorn Ku Qiao, Lotus sorcerer

Attributes: Bod 5, Chi 0 (Mag 8), Mnd 6, Ref 6
Skills: Info/Lotus Hierarchy 8, Martial Arts 10, Sorcery 15
Schticks: Blast (Acid, Fire, Ice), Divination

any other target they wish). Mang Ri will stand his ground until he receives 1 point of impairment. Then Blood of Flames attacks the PCs, allowing Mang Ri to escape. Again, Five Pains will fight at Mang Ri's side, but halfheartedly.

Blood of Flames, typical named fire demon

Attributes: Bod 8, Chi 4, Mnd 7, Ref 7
Skills: Creature Abilities 16, Martial Arts 17
Schticks: Burning Blood (see p. 95), Blast (fire), Regeneration (x2)
Damage: 13 (sword), 18 (blast)
Notes: Blood of Flames and his five brothers appear as burning, ape–like creatures. Their faces flicker through various states of agony as they sweep across the ice, slicing out with their swords of fire. Blood of Flames must remain cautious during this fight. If he stays in one place too long, he will melt through the ice and drown.

COMPLICATIONS

- Obviously, with this much fire flying about the ice is bound to grow weak. Much of the imperial army will fall through holes deliberately burnt by the defenders. Likewise, Mang Ri and the Demons may throw fireblasts in the path of the PCs. If the PCs are using snowmobiles, they must make a Drive check (Difficulty 10, 1 shot) or the snowmobile splashes into the water and sinks to the bottom. The PC must then make a Martial Arts check (Difficulty 10, 1 shot), to grab onto the edge of the ice. Otherwise, they sink beneath the surface.
- PCs can make their own holes in the ice using magic or clever gunfire. Accept any reasonable suggestion for how to do this — yes, shooting a bunch of holes in the ice in cut-along-the-dotted-line style will work just fine.
- Any PCs who fall into the water automatically gain 1 point of Impairment from the cold. If they do not get warm and dry within an hour, they will begin taking 10 points of damage per hour until they die.
- PCs who sink under the surface must make a Perception check to find an opening (3 Shots, Difficulty 6). Alternatively, they may try to break a new hole in the ice. The ice has a Dodge and Toughness of 5. Meanwhile, the character takes damage from drowning.
- Eventually, the ice will grow very unstable. It will begin to crack and shift underfoot. All combatants need to make three Martial Arts checks to reach safety (3 Shots, Difficulty 8).
- The Blizzard, once begun, will reduce all vision to three meters. Bows become useless. Guns are only effective at point-blank range. Communication becomes virtually impossible. All damage from cold (e.g. characters who went swimming) is doubled. The imperial army rapidly deteriorates.

THE END

If the PCs haven't already launched a plan of their own once the blizzard hits, Ku Qiao will suggest that the remains of the imperial army attack the temple, providing a diversion as the PCs sneak inside. With the weather eliminating bow combat, all the guards move to defend the first floor. Meanwhile, Mang Ri rushes about the main hallway shouting orders.

Unless the PCs botch their entry rolls, they should reach him without any significant encounters. If they do trip over a rock or something, a handful of soldiers engage them in combat and Mang Ri and Five Pains come running to see what the shouting is about.

Once Mang Ri is on the scene, or once the PCs find him and attack, eight guards arrive each sequence for as long as the GM desires. Five Pains simply hovers nearby, watching. Mang Ri screams for assistance from his demonic servant. "Five Pains, destroy them! I am your master. I order you to attack!"

But Five Pains simply laughs. "Poor fool — your death is my freedom. This has all happened according to my plan." He then vanishes through the floor.

FALLOUT

Once Mang Ri dies, the imperial army bursts through the defenses and the remaining guards surrender. Mang Ri's soul will descend to the Underworld and Five Pains will be free. However, unless at least three PCs have died during the adventure then Five Pains will find himself tied to the Underworld by his debt to Horns of Fire. Since his freedom depends on the PCs' deaths, he will continue to harass them and their associates. Benjamin Franklin Smith is likely to have the same idea.

If the PCs capture Mang Ri without killing him, Ku Qiao takes the renegade back to Lo-yang in chains. Mang Ri is executed — but since he does not die in battle, he does not take Five Pains' place in the Underworld. Five Pains remains shackled to hell, but vows to revenge himself on the PCs. This is a plan his demonic lords readily approve of, and they send him back to the contemporary juncture.

Finally, Fire Thorn Ku Qiao owes the PCs a debt for helping to remove the renegade Lotus agent. He even awards the party a Jade Leaf (a Lotus mark of debt). Of course, after his success here the Petals soon promote him to an assignment in the contemporary juncture. Inevitably, he and the PCs will meet again — this time as enemies. In the meantime, however, Ku can provide some answers to the PCs' questions. And so, the story continues.

Index

Ars Magica

Welcome to a land of adventure and mystery, of falling empires and rising nations, of legendary creatures and myths. This is **Ars Magica's** Mythic Europe, where magic exists alongside the history of the Middle Ages.

The glories of the Classical world are dust and the promise of the Renaissance is yet to come. Life is a struggle: wars and plagues stalk the land, the Church and kings rule with an iron fist. Yet Mythic Europe is also a place of magical wonder: faeries and rural spirits must be placated; demons corrupt everything they touch; divine power is accessible through prayer; and magic is everywhere.

Against this backdrop, the magi of the Order of Hermes wield the magical Vis energy that pervades the world. You and your troupe seek arcane knowledge while taking the roles of magi, wizards of legendary power who are the leaders of the covenant. But you may also portray the loyal companions of the magi who use their professional skills for a share of the the reward; or you might play the grogs who stand with the magi as the stalwart guards of the covenant, leading lives far more exciting than those of the common folk. With each role you play you have knowledge few others possess. You know of **Ars Magica**, the Art of Magic.

BY JONATHAN TWEET AND MARK REIN • HAGEN

ARS MAGICA, 4TH EDITION HARDCOVER
AG0204HC
ISBN 1-887801-56-1

ATLAS GAMES

ARS MAGICA, 4TH EDITION SOFTCOVER
AG0204
ISBN 1-887801-55-3